AF484979

First published in the United States by
The Lighthouse Academy Press
Printed by Kindle Direct Publishing, USA
Additional copies for sale at Amazon Books

ISBN: 979-8-9953537-0-6

This work was developed through a human–AI collaboration. Draft materials were produced with the assistance of generative tools, after which the author revised, restructured, and refined all text for accuracy, coherence, and fidelity of voice. See *Author's Note.*

The cover was created using digital rendering tools.

# WAR AND REPUBLIC

*America's Drift from*

*Declaration to Perpetual Emergency*

## William J. Striker

# Contents

# Author's Note

I came to this subject before I had a theory about it — first feeling it as a pressure, and then as a question.

I was young during the last years of the Vietnam draft — not yet of draft age — and had no reason to assume the war would end before my number came up. Like many of my generation, I lived under the shadow of a war that was real in blood, real in fear, and real in consequence, yet somehow different in form from the wars that had shaped my parents' world. It was not merely that Vietnam was far away. It was that the nation had gone deeply into war, so soon after Korea, again without using the older constitutional language and public ritual that earlier generations associated with war itself. A new pattern of war was forming.

I remember one argument with my father. We almost never argued, which is perhaps why that moment remained with me. I told him that if I were drafted, I would go. He answered, with more force than I was used to hearing from him, "I'll send you off to Canada before I allow you to fight in that war." For a young man, that kind of statement has weight. For me, it had even more weight because it came from someone who belonged to an earlier American generation, a generation for whom the meaning of war had been marked by open attack, national assent, and formal commitment. He and my mother, both answering the national challenges of WWII, understood what it meant for a republic openly to commit itself.

It took me time to understand how much was carried in his answer. He was not speaking out of softness, cowardice, or indifference to national defense. He was speaking from a distinction that I only later learned to formulate properly: not every war is the same kind of constitutional act.

Years later, the subject returned to me in another form. The Iran–Contra affair was the first governance question I pursued in real depth. I read everything I could find on it — articles, hearings, books, reports, and the small, easily missed notices that often reveal actions behind each news headline. In that process I discovered the peculiar intellectual force of constitutional inquiry: the ability to see that a bland or cryptic public detail may imply an entire hidden structure of action beneath it. Once that faculty awakens, it does not easily go back to sleep.

This book grew out of that long experience of pressure becoming question, and question becoming study. Its subject is not war in the abstract, but war as a constitutional act in a republic: who decides, by what authority, under what visibility, at whose burden, and by what means the action ends. Those questions belong not only to scholars or officials, but to the constitutional life of the republic itself.

One additional word is appropriate about how this book was written.

Parts of the research, drafting, and structural development of this work were assisted by modern artificial intelligence tools. Those tools can help gather material, test arguments, and organize complex historical patterns in ways that were not previously possible. Yet the experience remains fundamentally human. The questions, the judgments about proportion, the interpretation of evidence, and the responsibility for the argument belong to the author.

If artificial intelligence played a role in the making of this book, it did so as a conversation partner and instrument, not as a substitute for the human act of historical understanding.

# Preface

War is one of the oldest tests of republican government.

It demands speed where republics prefer deliberation, unity where they prefer divided power, secrecy where they prefer visibility, and obedience where they prefer consent. Every republic must therefore solve the same problem: how to defend itself without allowing the instruments of defense to become the ordinary form of rule.

This book examines how the United States has attempted to answer that problem, and how that answer has changed over time.

It is not a catalogue of battles, though battles appear in it. It is not a legal treatise in the narrow sense, though constitutional argument runs through every chapter. And it is not a moral scorecard assigning simple praise or blame to each use of force. Some wars have been necessary. Some actions have plainly served national defense. Some have rested on broad public support. Others have been more doubtful in origin, murkier in form, or more elusive in their constitutional footing. Historical seriousness requires distinction. The aim of this book is to recover the distinctions too often passed over.

The subject here is **war as a constitutional act**.

Americans often speak of wars, interventions, police actions, authorizations, emergencies, covert operations, limited strikes, and national-security measures as though they were simply different labels for the same underlying thing. They are not. The words matter because the structure matters. A declared war, openly debated and publicly assumed, is not the same political event as a prolonged military action undertaken under broad authorization, sustained through appropriations, partially obscured by bureaucratic form, or distanced from the citizen through secrecy, contractors, debt, and a professional volunteer force.

The older constitutional vocabulary recognized that entering war was a grave public act. It carried legal consequences, political consequences, and civic consequences. Above all, it carried visibility. The people knew that the republic had committed itself. Congress knew it. The executive knew it. The burden, whether welcomed or resisted, was broadly understood to be national.

Modern practice has often been different. The United States has not ceased to use force. On the contrary, it has used force repeatedly — in forms ranging from declared war to undeclared war, from proxy struggle to covert action, from limited strike to prolonged expedition. What has changed is not the existence of war power, but increasingly its distribution, its visibility, and the public experience of its burden.

That change is the concern of this book.

A substantial literature already exists on presidential war power and the constitutional tensions surrounding it. Arthur Schlesinger Jr.'s *The Imperial Presidency* remains the classic warning about the growth of executive authority in the modern age. Louis Fisher and others have examined the constitutional history of war powers in detail. John Hart Ely's *War and Responsibility* sharpened the critique in the wake of Vietnam, while other works have explored the Declare War Clause, the War Powers Resolution, and the national security state that emerged after 1945.

These studies have illuminated important parts of the problem. What they have rarely attempted, however, is to follow the question across the entire arc of republican experience.

This book attempts that broader view.

It begins with the classical warnings of Greece and Rome, moves through the constitutional design of the American founding, examines the early practice of the presidency, and then traces the long evolution of war powers through the undeclared wars of the twentieth century, the War Powers Resolution, covert action, proxy conflict, the operational state, private force, and the narrowing of civic burden in the age of the all-volunteer military.

History is full of facts. What it often lacks are explanations that connect those facts without forcing them.

The argument of this book is therefore architectural. It concerns declaration and initiation, but also appropriation and acquiescence. It concerns Congress and the President, but also intelligence agencies, covert action, contractors, public assent, and the distribution of burden across the citizen body. It concerns not only how wars begin, but how they continue, how they are hidden or exposed, and how they end — or fail to end.

Two disciplines guided the writing of these pages.

The first is to prefer **history to slogan**. On questions of war and constitutional power, slogans come easily. They spare us the harder work of tracing institutions, statutes, precedents, evasions, rationales, and consequences across time. That harder work is necessary because the American system did not change all at once. It changed through accumulation: precedent upon precedent, emergency upon emergency, accommodation upon accommodation.

The second is to prefer **proportion to heat**. War invites moral passion, and not without reason. Yet passion alone can distort understanding as easily as it can sharpen it. The purpose of this book is therefore to present the historical record and the operating structure of government as clearly as possible, leaving room for judgment without allowing indignation to do the work of analysis.

The reader will encounter both familiar landmarks and less familiar ones: the founding settlement, the early presidents, the last declared wars, Korea, Vietnam, the War Powers Resolution, Nicaragua, Iran–Contra, the growth of covert action, the operational drift of national-security institutions, the rise of private force, and the narrowing of civic burden in the all-volunteer republic.

The appendices serve a related purpose. They gather statutes, declarations, authorizations, timelines, and inventories whose cumulative effect is difficult to appreciate when encountered only piecemeal. Some readers may find those materials as revealing as the main narrative.

A book of this kind must finally be written for the citizen, not only the specialist. War powers are not the private property of lawyers, officials, or historians. They belong to the constitutional life of the republic itself. They touch the legislator who votes, the executive who orders, the soldier who serves, the family that waits, the taxpayer who funds, and the citizen who must decide whether the nation still acts under law or increasingly under habit disguised as necessity.

That question has not become less important with time. It has become more important.

The United States remains powerful. It remains exposed to danger. It remains obliged to act in a difficult world. None of those realities removes the old republican problem. They intensify it.

For that reason, the subject of war powers should not be treated as an antiquarian dispute over clauses and phrases. It is a living question about whether a free government can preserve its own form while retaining the means to defend itself.

That is the question to which this book is addressed.

# War and Republic

# Introduction

*The Problem of War in a Republic*

A republic must possess war powers.

That much is unavoidable. No serious political order can survive if it lacks the power to defend itself, repel attack, suppress insurrection, secure its borders, and meet armed threats with force. The question, therefore, is not whether a republic may fight. The question is how a republic structures the authority to fight so that the instruments of defense do not become the ordinary form of rule.

The founders made the republic possible; the framers gave it form.

The distinction is not just historical; it is structural. It marks the difference between political inheritance and constitutional design, between the experience that produced the American experiment and the structure that was built to preserve it.

That problem is the permanent political problem to which this book is addressed.

War has always posed a special danger to free governments because it brings necessity to the surface. It compresses time, narrows deliberation, elevates command, excuses secrecy, and demands obedience. All governments feel that pressure in war. Republics feel it more sharply because their ordinary legitimacy depends not upon command alone, but upon law, consent, division of power, and civic accountability. A monarchy may more easily treat war as an extension of prerogative. A republic cannot do so without changing its own character.

The American Constitution was framed in full awareness of that difficulty. Where the founders inherited the problem, the framers did not attempt to abolish war power, for no nation could. They attempted instead to distribute it. Congress was given the power to declare war, raise and support armies, provide and maintain a navy, make rules for captures, govern the armed forces, call forth the militia, and, most crucially, control appropriations. The President was made Commander in Chief. That arrangement was neither accidental nor merely stylistic. It reflected a deliberate effort to combine energy with restraint: energy in defense and execution, restraint in the decision to place the nation into war.

The famous Convention change from the power to "make war" to the power to "declare war" has often been misunderstood. It did not vest a general authority to commence war in the executive. It preserved the executive's ability to repel sudden attacks while leaving the larger judgment of war to the legislature. In the founding design, the President was to command force; Congress was to decide when the republic would enter the condition of war, and Congress was also to hold the purse without which sustained war could not continue. The design assumed tension between branches, but it also assumed that this tension was a safeguard rather than a defect.

Yet constitutions do not live only in clauses. They live in practice, precedent, emergency, institutional habit, public psychology, and the slow pressure of events. Over time, the American system did not abandon war powers; it altered their working distribution. Formal declarations became rare. Presidential initiative became more frequent. Congressional participation often shifted from prior decision to later authorization, later acquiescence, or continued funding. The courts, for the most part, stood at a distance. Intelligence services, national-security staffs, covert channels, contractors, and multinational frameworks complicated the older picture still further. The legal vocabulary changed. So did the civic experience of war.

This change is best understood as a drift from declaration to perpetual emergency.

By **perpetual emergency** I do not mean that the United States has been in continuous combat at every moment, nor that every modern use of force is equivalent in scale or moral gravity. I mean something more structural: **a gradual normalization of the governing condition** in which emergency powers, arguments, habits, and institutions are no longer clearly exceptional. War or war-like force becomes easier to begin without declaration, easier to continue without renewed public assent, easier to sustain through narrower burdens, and easier to hide within specialized bureaucratic or legal forms.

That drift was not the product of a single coup, doctrine, or party. It did not arrive on one date. It emerged through accumulated episodes: early executive assertions, frontier precedents, civil-war necessity, the last great declared wars, the Cold War, Korea, Vietnam, legislative attempts at reassertion, the rise of covert action, the appropriation struggles of the 1970s and 1980s, the increasing role of intelligence and national-security bureaucracies, modern authorizations for the use of force, and the move from a citizen army with conscription to a professional volunteer force supported by technology, contractors, and debt.

To understand that history properly, one must look at more than formal legality. A republic's relation to war is shaped not only by who signs the order, but also by who bears the burden and how visible the burden remains. A war that is declared openly, debated publicly, funded explicitly, and fought in part by conscripted citizens is not the same kind of republican event as a war that is loosely authorized, debt-financed, fought by a professional minority, operationalized through specialized agencies, and only dimly present in the daily consciousness of most citizens. Both may involve real force. Both may be defended as necessary. But they do not bear equally upon the constitutional life of the republic.

For that reason, five governing questions recur throughout the analysis.

First, **authority**: by what claimed authority was force initiated, widened, or sustained?

Second, **assent**: what form of consent or authorization existed, whether formal declaration, statute, resolution, appropriations, or simply political acquiescence?

Third, **visibility**: how visible was the action to Congress and to the public?

Fourth, **burden**: how widely were the costs distributed, whether through conscription, taxes, debt, volunteer service, secrecy, or private contracting?

Fifth, **termination**: by what mechanism was force limited, ended, or brought back under ordinary constitutional control?

These questions guide the inquiry throughout the chapters that follow — not as a rigid template, but as disciplines of judgment, applied where the historical record requires them and accumulated across the narrative as a whole. They are meant to keep the inquiry honest and proportioned. Without them, the history of American war powers quickly dissolves either into a mere list of interventions or into abstract constitutional assertion detached from institutions and human cost.

The aim here is neither to celebrate nor to denounce American power in the abstract. It is not written to flatten every conflict into the same moral shape. Some wars were plainly necessary; some actions were clearly lawful; some were supported by overwhelming public conviction; some involved grave ambiguity; some rested on broad congressional authorization; some pressed heavily against constitutional limits; some appeared to evade them. Historical seriousness requires distinction. The purpose is to recover those distinctions where they have been blurred.

Accordingly, the analysis proceeds in five main movements.

The first part examines the inherited republican problem and the constitutional design by which the American founders sought to meet it. The second follows the early tests of that design in the actions of Washington, Jefferson, Jackson, and Lincoln. The third traces the great modern drift through the last declared wars, Korea, Vietnam, the War Powers Resolution, and the appropriations struggle. The fourth explores what may be called the shadow constitution of war: Nicaragua, Iran-Contra, covert action, intelligence operational drift, contractors, and the blurred line between war and policing. The fifth turns to the modern condition of perpetual emergency, asking how the language of authorization, the narrowing of civic burden, and the changing visibility of force altered the operating character of American government.

The appendices serve a related but different purpose. They provide the documentary and empirical scale that the narrative body cannot carry without losing shape. There the reader will find the constitutional texts, key founding and presidential documents, major war powers statutes, conscription and mobilization data, and a tiered inventory of American uses of force abroad, including selected documented covert operations. One of the quiet arguments lies in that inventory itself. When the actions are gathered in one place, the scale of activity becomes difficult to ignore.

The broad question, then, is simple to ask and difficult to answer.

Can a republic remain a republic while emergency becomes normal?

The American experience suggests neither a simple yes nor a simple no. It suggests something more troubling and more instructive. A republic may preserve its forms for a very long time while the operating meaning of those forms changes. It may continue to speak the language of divided power while initiative shifts. It may continue to invoke Congress while relying increasingly on after-the-fact assent. It may preserve elections and statutes while narrowing the public's felt share in the burden of war. It may remain constitutional in text while becoming more elastic in practice.

This book follows that elasticity.

Its central contention is that the most important constitutional change in American war powers has not been the open abolition of old restraints, but the gradual lowering of political and institutional friction in the use of force. War became easier to enter without declaration, easier to sustain without shared burden, easier to conduct through specialized channels, and easier to defend as temporary even when its emergency logic endured.

A republic can fight. It must.

Whether it can fight indefinitely without becoming something looser, more executive, more opaque, and less fully republican in operation is the question to which the rest of this book is addressed.

# Part I:
# Inheritance and Design

# Chapter 1:
## Guardians, Dictators, and Citizens

The problem of war in a republic is far older than the American Constitution. It is as old as political reflection itself. Every free state must answer the same hard question: how is a people to defend itself without allowing the instruments of defense to become the principle of rule?

Plato confronted that problem in the *Republic* by way of the guardian. Once the just city has been described in outline, Socrates is compelled to ask what sort of men will preserve it. The city must have defenders; it must therefore train a class capable of courage, discipline, and force. Yet this immediately creates a danger. The very qualities that make men formidable in war may render them dangerous in peace. A guardian who is fierce enough to face an enemy may also become fierce toward his own people.[1]

Plato's answer is not sentimental. He does not pretend that the city can be defended by softness. The guardian must be swift, strong, spirited, and brave. But spirit alone is not enough. The guardian must also possess a contrary quality: he must be gentle toward those he is meant to protect. Socrates reaches for the famous image of the well-bred dog, fierce toward strangers and enemies, yet gentle toward those it knows.[2] The image is memorable because it names the central political paradox. A republic must arm itself, but it must not make savagery its ruling virtue.

---

[1]  Plato, *Republic*, trans. Benjamin Jowett, II.375a–375e.
[2]  Plato, *Republic*, II.375a–376a.

Plato then presses farther. The true guardian, he says, must possess something of the philosopher, because he distinguishes friend from enemy by the criterion of knowledge and ignorance.[3] Force, in other words, must not become self-directing. The class trained for war must remain subordinate to reason. The guardian is not to rule by the mere fact that he can strike; he is to serve an order whose ends lie above violence.

That insight is one of the deep inheritances of classical political thought. Plato understood that constitutions are not only arrangements of offices. They arise from the character of the men who compose them. In one of the most penetrating lines of the *Republic*, he says that states do not grow out of "oak and rock," but out of the human natures within them.[4] Political order is therefore inseparable from moral formation. A city in which spirit outruns reason will not remain what it was, whatever its laws may say.

This is why Plato's analysis of tyranny matters so much for any later republic. In Book VIII, as democracy degenerates into tyranny, Socrates describes the tyrant as one who must keep the people dependent upon leadership by fear. "The tyrant," he says, "must be always getting up a war, in order that the people may require a leader."[5] That sentence goes directly to the heart of the political question before us. War is not only an external danger. It can become an internal instrument: a means of preserving command by preserving emergency. Plato's warning is not that every war produces tyranny. It is that war can create conditions favorable to tyranny, especially when a people grows accustomed to being governed through danger.

---

[3]  Plato, *Republic*, II.376a–376c.
[4]  Plato, *Republic*, VIII.544d–544e.
[5]  Plato, *Republic*, VIII.566e–567a.

Rome approached the same problem differently. Where Plato thought first in terms of the soul and the order of the city, Rome thought in magistracies, terms of office, and constitutional forms. It was less philosophical, more institutional, more practical. Yet it faced the same essential difficulty: how to preserve a republic that would need force, generals, and emergency command.

Later, Polybius would praise Rome's constitution as a mixed order, combining monarchical, aristocratic, and popular elements.[6] That praise mattered because the Romans themselves had, over time, fashioned a practical answer to the problem of balance. They did not attempt to abolish concentrated authority altogether. They tried instead to limit and distribute it.

The clearest Roman device for doing so was the dictatorship. In moments of grave danger the ordinary magistracies might be too slow. The republic therefore permitted the appointment of a dictator with concentrated power. Yet, in its earlier and healthier form, that office was exceptional, temporary, and bounded by purpose. It existed not to replace the republic, but to preserve it in emergency.

The old Roman ideal appears with unusual force in Livy's account of Lucius Quinctius Cincinnatus. The envoys of the Senate find him across the Tiber, working his four-acre farm. He is asked to put on his toga and receive the state's command, because he is now "the sole hope of the Roman people."[7] In that scene the Roman mind reveals itself. The man called to

---

6   Polybius, *Histories*, VI.11–18. For a useful modern summary of Polybius on Rome's mixed constitution and dictatorship, see Will Durant, *Caesar and Christ* (New York: Simon and Schuster, 1944), chap. II.

7   Livy, *The History of Rome*, trans. D. Spillan (London: Henry G. Bohn, 1853), III.26.

supreme power is not one already enthroned in splendor, but a citizen summoned from labor.

More important still is what follows. Cincinnatus acts swiftly, relieves the trapped Roman force, defeats the enemy, and then lays down the dictatorship after only sixteen days, though it had been granted for six months.[8] That voluntary renunciation is the heart of the story. Emergency power is not denied; it is limited by time, purpose, and civic expectation. Rome at its best understood that concentrated authority may sometimes be necessary, but it ceases to be republican when it becomes normal.

From Plato and Rome together, then, a double warning emerges. Plato warns against the political ascendancy of the guardian principle itself. Rome warns against the institutional normalization of emergency power. The one danger is moral and psychological; the other is constitutional and political. Yet they are closely allied. A republic is endangered when those trained for force cease to remain subordinate to civic reason, and when temporary command ceases to remain temporary.

The late Roman Republic demonstrated how these boundaries could fail. The old forms survived, but their operating character began to change. The Republic still had magistrates, assemblies, and senatorial dignity; yet military command, personal loyalty, and emergency precedents increasingly outweighed the old balance. Civil conflict had become so destructive that, as Plutarch reports in his *Life of Caesar*, some men concluded the commonwealth was "incurable but by a monarchy."[9] That is one of the most revealing sentences in the entire Roman story. It marks the moment when

---

[8] Livy, *History of Rome*, III.27–29.
[9] Plutarch, "Caesar," in *Lives*, trans. Bernadotte Perrin, sec. 28.

emergency ceases to be seen as an exception and begins to be rationalized as regime.

Caesar's career completed the lesson. Plutarch's account does not need to be treated either as partisan invective or as unquestionable gospel; but on this point it is unmistakably clear. When Caesar was made dictator for life, Plutarch writes, "this was indeed a tyranny avowed, since his power now was not only absolute, but perpetual too."[10] There the old Roman emergency office ceased to be what it had once claimed to be. Its form remained, but its limit vanished. The republic had not simply suffered a military defeat; it had been altered from within by the changed meaning of command.

This is why the Roman example reaches so deeply into later constitutional thought. A republic does not perish only when it is conquered by a foreign enemy. It may also be deformed by its own methods of self-preservation. The offices remain; the language remains; the ceremonies remain. Yet the distribution of real power changes, and the habits of obedience change with it.

The classical inheritance, then, was not a set of distant examples admired only by scholars. It was a body of political experience that later republics studied with care. The founders of the American Republic knew the Greek and Roman histories well. They had read Plato, Livy, Plutarch, and Polybius; they understood that republics must sometimes fight, and that emergency authority may sometimes be necessary. But they also understood the darker lesson those histories carried: that the concentration of military and political power, even when justified by necessity, had repeatedly altered or destroyed republican government.

---

[10]  Plutarch, "Caesar," in *Lives*, sec. 57.

The American Constitution was therefore framed in the shadow of that problem.

The founders did not attempt to abolish war powers, for no nation could safely do so. Instead they attempted something more difficult. They divided those powers. They placed the authority to declare war and control the public purse in the legislature, while entrusting the command of the armed forces to the executive. The intention was not merely procedural. It was to ensure that the republic would enter war deliberately, not easily, and that the instruments of defense would remain subordinate to the civil order.

Whether that design held — and how it changed over time — is the subject to which we now turn.

# Chapter 2:
# A Constitution for War and Peace

When the delegates assembled in Philadelphia in 1787, they did not approach the question of war power as a theoretical exercise. They approached it as students of history.

They knew the Greek and Roman warnings. They knew that republics could be undone not only by foreign enemies, but by the domestic consequences of military command and prolonged emergency. They also knew something nearer and more practical: they had just lived through a failed constitutional experiment. The Articles of Confederation had preserved American independence, but they had not provided a durable architecture for common defense, common finance, or common rule. Congress could deliberate and decide about war and peace, but it depended on the states for money, men, and execution. It could resolve; it could request; it could recommend. It could not reliably command.[11]

That weakness mattered in war, but it mattered no less in peace. A union that could not act with steadiness in external affairs, raise resources with regularity, or speak with sufficient authority in matters touching national safety was not likely to remain secure for long. The lesson the founders drew was not that republican government had failed. It was that a republic required a stronger and more coherent constitutional structure than the Confederation had provided.

---

[11] Articles of Confederation of 1781, arts. VIII–IX; *The Federalist* No. 15 (Alexander Hamilton).

Yet the solution was not to gather all power into one set of hands. The delegates did not come to Philadelphia seeking a king in republican dress. They meant to create a government strong enough to defend the nation, but not so simple in structure that war could become the private instrument of a single will. The constitutional problem was therefore double. The new government had to possess energy. It also had to possess restraint.

That double purpose explains much of the Constitution's design. The document was not framed for peace alone, nor for war alone, but for the alternation of both. It assumes that danger will sometimes require force, and that force will require coordination, finance, command, and law. But it also assumes that in a republic such powers must be distributed, reviewed, and politically answerable. The Constitution's treatment of war is therefore not contained in a single clause. It is an architecture.

The clearest evidence of that architecture is found in Article I. Congress is given the power to declare war, grant letters of marque and reprisal, raise and support armies, provide and maintain a navy, make rules concerning captures on land and water, make rules for the government and regulation of the land and naval forces, call forth the militia to execute the laws, suppress insurrections, and repel invasions, and organize, arm, and discipline that militia.[12] Taken together, these powers show that the legislative role in war was never meant to be ceremonial. Congress was not simply to announce a conflict already made by others. It was to decide, authorize, sustain, regulate, and in a material sense constitute the nation's war-making capacity.

That point is often obscured when attention is fixed exclusively on the phrase "declare war." Important as that phrase is, it is only one part of a larger constitutional cluster. The

---

[12]  U.S. Const. art. I, sec. 8, cls. 11–16.

founders did not treat war as a discrete royal prerogative transferred wholesale to one department. They broke it into parts. One institution was given the power to authorize and fund; another was given the power to command and execute; both were left to operate under law.

This is why the appropriations provisions are so important. Congress was not simply empowered to raise and support armies; it was expressly forbidden to appropriate money to that use for a term longer than two years.[13] The significance of that limitation should not be understated. A standing military force, if it were to continue, had to be brought repeatedly back under legislative review. The Constitution thus denied permanence to military funding even while allowing national military power. The same logic appears in the broader Appropriations Clause: "No Money shall be drawn from the Treasury, but in Consequence of Appropriations made by Law."[14] War, if sustained, would have to pass through the legislature not once, but continuously.

This was not legislative fussiness. It was constitutional design. A republic that fears both foreign danger and domestic domination must ensure that armed force remains dependent on recurring civic consent. In that sense the power of the purse was not an accessory to the war power. It was one of its central restraints.

At the same time, the founders were not so naïve as to suppose that military operations could be directed by a deliberative assembly. Whatever the political decision to fight, armies still required unity in movement and command. This is where Article II enters the picture. The President is made "Commander in Chief of the Army and Navy of the United States, and of the Militia of the several States, when called into

---

[13]   U.S. Const. art. I, sec. 8, cl. 12.
[14]   U.S. Const. art. I, sec. 9, cl. 7.

the actual Service of the United States."[15] The office is one of command, not of legislative constitution. Its purpose is to provide vigor, dispatch, and unity in execution once force exists and is lawfully engaged.

Hamilton later defended this principle in *The Federalist*, arguing that the direction of war "most peculiarly demands those qualities which distinguish the exercise of power by a single hand."[16] The point was not monarchic; it was functional. A military campaign cannot be conducted by committee. A republic may insist on legislative judgment before war and legislative support during war, yet still require executive unity in command.

The Constitution therefore embodies a deliberate asymmetry. It does not divide everything evenly. It allocates according to function. Congress is given the powers most closely associated with entering, structuring, and sustaining war; the President is given the power most closely associated with directing it. The arrangement is not tidy in the abstract, but it is intelligible in practice. Deliberation and funding are diffused. Command is unified.

That same logic helps explain the militia clauses, which are often noticed but not always taken seriously enough. The founders did not intend the American republic to rely exclusively on a permanent professional army detached from civil society. Congress could call forth the militia to execute the laws, suppress insurrections, and repel invasions, and could provide for organizing, arming, and disciplining it; yet the states retained the appointment of officers and the authority of training according to the discipline prescribed by Congress.[17] Here again the design

---

[15] U.S. Const. art. II, sec. 2, cl. 1.

[16] *The Federalist* No. 74 (Alexander Hamilton).

[17] U.S. Const. art. I, sec. 8, cls. 15–16.

is mixed. National necessity is acknowledged, but local and civic elements are preserved. The militia was part of the constitutional answer to the old republican fear that a free people might become dependent upon a standing military establishment alone.

The inclusion of letters of marque and reprisal points in the same direction. To modern readers the clause seems archaic, but in the eighteenth century it was entirely practical. It allowed Congress to authorize limited private force against enemy commerce, a practice long familiar in European warfare.[18] More important for constitutional understanding, it shows that even irregular or delegated forms of hostilities were treated as legislative matters. The initiation of lawful violence, whether carried out by public armies or licensed private actors, was not left to executive discretion alone. It was to pass through public authority.

Hamilton's argument in *Federalist* No. 23 gives the broadest rationale for the whole structure. The circumstances that threaten the safety of nations, he wrote, are "infinite," and no constitutional system can wisely deny the government the means necessary for common defense.[19] This is a crucial point. The framers were not designing a pacifist constitution. They were designing a strong republic, and strength requires capacity. But capacity under the Constitution was never meant to mean simplicity. The government had to be able to act, but it was to act through distributed powers and reciprocal checks.

---

[18]  The United States Constitution, Article I, Section 8, Clause 11, grants Congress the power "to declare War, grant Letters of Marque and Reprisal." Privateering was formally abolished among most European powers by the Declaration of Paris (1856), which the United States declined to sign. The constitutional power therefore technically remains part of American law, though it has not been exercised in modern times. The historical implications of this clause — and its modern echoes in private military contracting — are discussed in Chapter 15.

[19]  *The Federalist* No. 23 (Alexander Hamilton).

The Constitution was not framed to eliminate war powers. No serious nation could do that. It was framed to divide them. The distinction matters because later debate has often proceeded as though the only real question were whether the President or Congress "has" the war power. That way of speaking is misleading from the start. The Constitution does not confer a single undivided war power upon either branch. It builds an interlocking system. Congress has the power to authorize, raise, fund, and regulate; the President has the power to command; both stand within a larger constitutional order in which the people, through representation, bear the burdens and judge the use of force politically over time.

This arrangement did not guarantee harmony. It was not meant to. The founders knew enough history to distrust harmony purchased by concentration of power. What they hoped to produce instead was friction before decision, energy in execution, and dependence on law throughout. A republic, in their view, should not enter war by impulse, still less by prerogative. It should enter war by public act, under institutions capable of both force and restraint.

The architecture was therefore strong, but not simple. It answered the classical problem only up to a point. It established the broad distribution of powers. It did not settle every future question about their boundary. Indeed, one of the most revealing debates still remained. The Convention first placed in Congress the power to "make" war, and later altered the phrase to "declare" war.[20] That change has carried more constitutional weight than its brevity might suggest.

---

[20] James Madison, Notes of Debates in the Federal Convention of 1787, Aug. 17, 1787.

The Constitution for war and peace was now in view. The question that remains is why the Convention ultimately chose the phrase "declare war" rather than "make war," and what the founders meant that distinction to preserve.

# Chapter 3:
# Declare, Make, and Repel Sudden Attacks

By the summer of 1787, the Convention had largely settled the broad architecture of the new government.[21] Congress would possess the legislative powers necessary for national defense: the authority to raise armies, provide a navy, regulate the armed forces, and control the national purse. The President would command those forces once they existed. What remained was a narrower but revealing question: how the Constitution would describe the legislature's authority to place the republic into war. The Committee of Detail had given Congress the power to make war. When the clause came before the Convention on August 17, the wording was reconsidered. The change that followed was brief but consequential.

Pierce Butler wanted to go further in the opposite direction. He proposed vesting the power in the President, arguing that the executive would have the necessary qualities and would not make war unless the nation supported it.[22] That suggestion brought the underlying issue into the open. The Convention was no longer debating mere wording. It was deciding whether the power to initiate war would be entrusted to a representative legislature or to a single magistrate.

Madison and Gerry answered Butler by moving "to insert 'declare,' striking out 'make' war; leaving to the Executive the power to repel sudden attacks."[23] The sentence is brief, but few

---

[21] James Madison, Notes of Debates in the Federal Convention of 1787, July–August 1787.

[22] Madison, *Notes of Debates*, Aug. 17, 1787.

[23] Madison, *Notes of Debates*, Aug. 17, 1787. See also *Constitution Annotated*, Art. I, sec. 8, cl. 11.

sentences in the records of the Convention have carried more constitutional weight. It reveals, in compressed form, the line the framers were trying to draw. They did not mean to make the executive helpless in the face of immediate danger. A republic could not wait upon leisurely forms when invasion or attack required instant resistance. Yet neither did they mean to transfer to the executive a general authority to commence war.

Roger Sherman objected to the change because he feared that "declare" might narrow Congress's authority too much. In Madison's notes, Sherman remarked that the executive should be able "to repel and not to commence war," and thought that "make" might state the legislative power more fully. That objection is important. It shows that those who preferred the older wording did so to preserve the fullness of legislative authority, and yet still maintained that the executive should be able only "to repel and not to commence war." They did not envision an executive right to begin war at pleasure. The disagreement was over precision, not over whether the President could assume the British king's prerogative.

Gerry's response, returning to Butler's proposal, was sharper. He said he "never expected to hear in a republic a motion to empower the Executive alone to declare war."[24] That sentence belongs to the political heart of the Convention. To place the war decision in one office was, in Gerry's view, alien to the very character of the regime they were creating.

Oliver Ellsworth then gave the debate a form that has echoed through American constitutional discussion ever since. There was, he said, "a material difference between the cases of making war, and making peace." It should be "more easy to get out of war, than into it."[25] George Mason pressed the same

---

[24] Madison, *Notes*, Aug. 17, 1787.
[25] Madison, *Notes*, Aug. 17, 1787.

principle more bluntly. He was against giving the power of war to the executive, because the executive was not safely to be trusted with it; and against giving it to the Senate, because that body was not so constituted as to deserve it. He was for "clogging rather than facilitating war," while facilitating peace.[26]

Those remarks reveal the true logic of the change. The substitution of "declare" for "make" did not turn Congress into a ceremonial announcer of wars already begun by the President. It did not empty the legislature's authority into diplomatic formality. It narrowed the wording to preserve a small but necessary sphere of executive defense, while leaving the political judgment of war where the framers believed it belonged: in the legislature.

The distinction was narrow, but consequential. To repel is not to commence.

That line is often lost in later argument. Some readers seize upon the word "declare" and inferred that the President may therefore make war so long as Congress need only pronounce upon it afterward. Others assume that if the President may act suddenly in defense, then he possesses some broad undefined residue of offensive authority. Neither inference fits the debate itself. Madison and Gerry did not move to empower the President to begin war. They moved to preserve his ability to meet sudden attack without waiting for Congress to assemble, while withholding from him the larger authority to place the republic into war as a matter of policy.

Hamilton later confirmed the same constitutional line in *The Federalist*. In No. 69, contrasting the American President with the British king, he wrote that the President's authority "would amount to nothing more than the supreme command and

---

[26] Madison, *Notes*, Aug. 17, 1787. Mason was for "clogging rather than facilitating war; but for facilitating peace."

direction of the military and naval forces," whereas the king's authority extended to "the DECLARING of war and to the RAISING and REGULATING of fleets and armies," all of which, under the Constitution, would "appertain to the legislature."[27] No sentence more plainly states the intended inferiority of the American executive to the British monarch in matters of war.

Hamilton reinforced the executive side of the arrangement in No. 74. "The direction of war," he wrote, "most peculiarly demands those qualities which distinguish the exercise of power by a single hand."[28] This was not a contradiction, but a complement. Congress was to decide the public question of war. The President was to direct the common strength once war, or lawful military action, was underway. Judgment and command were not identical powers.

That distinction helps explain why the Constitution can assign Congress the war decision while still naming the President Commander in Chief. The Commander in Chief Clause does not swallow Article I. It presupposes that forces have been raised, supported, and brought into service under law. The President commands what the Constitution and Congress have made available. He does not thereby acquire the British king's prerogative Hamilton took such pains to deny him.[29]

Madison later stated the same principle in even sterner language. Writing to Jefferson in 1798, he observed that "The constitution supposes, what the History of all Govts demonstrates, that the Ex. is the branch of power most interested in war, & most prone to it. It has accordingly with

---

[27] Alexander Hamilton, *The Federalist* No. 69.

[28] Hamilton, *The Federalist* No. 74.

[29] U.S. Const. art. II, sec. 2, cl. 1; Hamilton, *The Federalist* No. 69.

studied care, vested the question of war in the Legisl."[30] That is not a casual comment made long after the fact. It is one of the clearest retrospective statements from a leading founder about what the Constitution was designed to do.

The importance of the declare-for-make change therefore lies not in verbal subtlety alone, but in constitutional structure. The founders were trying to preserve three things at once: legislative control over the political decision for war, executive power to meet sudden attack, and executive unity in military command once force was lawfully engaged. The wording was chosen not to blur those lines, but to keep them from collapsing into one another.

There was, to be sure, no expectation that every future controversy would disappear. The boundary between defense and initiation, between sudden attack and planned hostilities, between command and policy, would prove difficult in practice. The founders knew enough history to understand that parchment could not answer every case in advance. What they did provide was a principle: the executive might act with speed in defense, but the decision to place the republic into war was meant to remain a legislative judgment.

That principle would be tested almost immediately. It would be tested by the early presidents, by events at sea, by frontier violence, by civil war, by undeclared wars, and by the growth of executive habit. The Constitution had drawn the line. American history would show how men honored it, stretched it, or crossed it.

---

[30] James Madison to Thomas Jefferson, Apr. 2, 1798, in *The Founders' Constitution*, vol. 3, art. I, sec. 8, cl. 11, doc. 8.

# Part II:
# Early American Tests

# Chapter 4:
# Washington and the Discipline of Peace

The Constitution had drawn the line. The first great test of that line did not come in a declared war, but in the effort to avoid one.

That fact is worth pausing over. The constitutional problem of war power is often imagined as a question that arises only when a president wishes to fight. Yet the earliest practical test came when the United States was pressed by events abroad, by faction at home, and by prior commitments into deciding whether it would remain at peace. In that setting, Washington's conduct mattered not simply because it was prudent, but because it helped reveal the distinction between preserving peace and placing the republic into war.

In 1793 the French Revolution had entered a more dangerous phase, and war had broken out between France and Great Britain, together with other European powers.[31] This created a genuine difficulty for the United States. The young republic was weak, divided, indebted, and militarily unprepared. More than that, it had a treaty relationship with France dating from 1778, forged in the struggle for American independence.[32] The issue was therefore not merely sentimental, though sentiment was strong. Many Americans felt gratitude toward

---

[31] The war that broke out in Europe in 1793 placed the United States under immediate pressure to choose its posture toward Revolutionary France and Great Britain. See Office of the Historian, "The Citizen Genêt Affair, 1793–1794."

[32] The United States had entered into a Treaty of Alliance with France on February 6, 1778. See National Archives, "Treaty of Alliance with France (1778)," and Office of the Historian, "French Alliance."

France and hostility toward Britain. But gratitude, memory, and faction did not answer the constitutional question.

Washington chose to treat the matter as one of national preservation.

On April 22, 1793, he issued what is commonly called the Proclamation of Neutrality. The document stated that "the duty and interest of the United States require, that they should with sincerity and good faith adopt and pursue a conduct friendly and impartial toward the belligerent Powers."[33] The language is important. Washington did not declare war. He did not even declare neutrality in the later statutory sense.[34] He announced the present policy and legal posture of the United States and warned citizens against acts inconsistent with it. The proclamation was at once diplomatic and executive: diplomatic in the position it announced to foreign powers, executive in the warning that the laws incident to that position would be enforced.

That distinction helps explain why Washington's act caused immediate controversy. He had not asked Congress for a declaration, because he was not asking Congress to enter war. Yet neither was he only issuing a social suggestion. He was acting from the executive office in foreign relations and law execution, and in doing so he established a practical precedent: the President might move first to preserve peace, proclaim the nation's impartial posture, and warn citizens against conduct that would drag the republic into hostilities.

---

[33] George Washington, "A Proclamation," Apr. 22, 1793.

[34] Although commonly called the "Proclamation of Neutrality," Washington's proclamation of April 22, 1793 does not use the word neutrality. Instead it states that the United States would pursue "a conduct friendly and impartial toward the belligerent Powers." Congress had not yet enacted neutrality legislation; the statutory framework governing neutrality violations would first appear in the Neutrality Act of 1794. Washington therefore announced the nation's diplomatic posture and warned citizens against acts inconsistent with it, rather than issuing a formal legal declaration of neutrality.

What Washington did not do is just as important. He did not claim a general authority to commence war. He did not say that the executive might decide the whole question of war and peace at pleasure. His act was narrower and more disciplined. It presumed peace until the constitutional authorities changed that condition. In that sense, the proclamation stood on the line that had been drawn at Philadelphia: the executive might act with speed in a matter touching foreign danger, yet the larger political question of war remained distinct from such executive initiative.

The Genêt affair put that line under severe pressure. Edmond Charles Genêt, the French minister sent to the United States, arrived in Charleston in April 1793 and almost immediately began issuing privateering commissions and attempting to enlist American support for French operations against British shipping. [35] In effect, he behaved as though popular enthusiasm and treaty memory could override the declared policy of the American government. He appealed over the administration's head to public feeling, and in doing so converted a difficult foreign-policy question into a direct test of American sovereignty.

Washington's response was firm. His administration treated Genêt's conduct as incompatible with the nation's neutral posture, and the affair eventually ended in Genêt's recall. More important for constitutional development, the crisis forced the United States to develop practical procedures for neutrality. [36]

---

[35]  Office of the Historian, "The Citizen Genêt Affair, 1793–1794." Genêt attempted to implement provisions of the 1778 Franco-American alliance by issuing privateering commissions and outfitting vessels in American ports.

[36]  Ibid. The controversy led the Washington administration to establish practical neutrality procedures, including the denial of such commissions, restrictions on arming belligerent ships in U.S. harbors, and the assertion of federal authority over prize and neutrality disputes. These practices were later codified in the Neutrality Act of 1794.

Here again Washington's conduct is instructive. He did not respond by placing the nation into war, nor by surrendering the government's judgment to popular excitement in favor of France. He insisted that foreign relations, however emotionally charged, remain subject to national authority and legal order.

The proclamation itself might have remained only an act of prudence had it not provoked a deeper constitutional debate. It did so almost immediately in the famous exchange between Hamilton and Madison writing as Pacificus and Helvidius. Their dispute is one of the earliest and most revealing constitutional arguments in American history because it showed how quickly a practical executive act could generate rival theories of executive power.

Hamilton's argument, in *Pacificus* No. 1, gave the strongest possible defense of Washington's step. The executive, he wrote, had the duty "to preserve peace till war is declared," and in fulfilling that duty it must necessarily judge the obligations imposed by treaties and enforce the laws incident to the nation's peaceful state.[37] Hamilton thus treated the proclamation as a lawful executive act precisely because it did not make war. It preserved peace, announced the nation's condition, and warned citizens that the obligations of neutrality would be enforced. In that narrower form, his defense fit well with Washington's actual conduct.

But Hamilton did not stop there. He also argued more broadly that such authority belonged "of course" to the Executive, and he connected it to the executive role in receiving ministers and judging the operative consequences of foreign

---

[37] Alexander Hamilton, *Pacificus* No. 1 (June 29, 1793). Hamilton argued that "it is on the other the duty of the Executive to preserve peace till war is declared," and that the proclamation properly announced the nation's condition and the enforcement of the laws incident to neutrality.

revolution and treaty relations.[38] This was the beginning of a larger theory of executive power in foreign affairs — one that reached beyond the immediate prudence of the proclamation itself.

Madison's response in *Helvidius* No. 1 was one of the most important constitutional protests ever written. He attacked not just the proclamation, but Hamilton's underlying doctrine. "The natural province of the executive magistrate," Madison wrote, "is to execute laws, as that of the legislature is to make laws."

Madison feared that Hamilton's reasoning, if accepted broadly, might allow the executive to shape the nation's war posture indirectly. If the President could determine neutrality and treaty obligations as matters of executive authority, that logic might gradually extend to the larger question of war itself.

"A declaration that there shall be war," Madison continued, "is not an execution of laws"; it is "one of the most deliberative acts that can be performed." From this he drew the larger conclusion that the war power is legislative in nature, not executive, and that to treat it as an executive power would confound the Constitution's separation of departments.

In *Helvidius,* Madison therefore insisted that the Constitution had placed the power of declaring war expressly in Congress, "where every other legislative power is declared to be vested."[39] He was not disputing that the President executed policy, received ministers, or acted as the nation's diplomatic organ. He was resisting the transformation of those powers into something approaching the old monarchical prerogative.

---

[38]  Ibid.

[39]  James Madison, *Helvidius* No. 1 (Aug. 24, 1793). Madison wrote that "The natural province of the executive magistrate is to execute laws," while a declaration of war "is one of the most deliberative acts that can be performed," and that the power of declaring war is "expressly vested in the Congress."

What is striking, and often missed, is that Washington's own conduct remained narrower than Hamilton's most expansive reasoning. The first President acted with resolution, but also with discipline. He did not behave as though the executive could simply determine war and peace. He acted to keep the peace while the nation remained legally at peace. He enforced a position of impartiality; he did not claim a right to put the republic into war without Congress. The practical precedent was therefore more restrained than the theory later advanced in its defense.

This is one reason Washington is so central to the constitutional tradition of war power. He demonstrated that executive energy need not be identical with executive aggrandizement. A republic might require prompt presidential action in foreign affairs without conceding to the President the authority to initiate war. The line was delicate, but it was not imaginary.

Washington's Farewell Address carried the same lesson into broader political reflection. He warned not only against "habitual hatred" and "habitual fondness" toward foreign nations, but also against the danger that such passions would make a nation "in some degree a slave." He cautioned that governments might be impelled into war "contrary to the best calculations of policy," or might make national animosity serve "projects of hostility instigated by pride, ambition, and other sinister and pernicious motives."[40] This was not isolationist fantasy. It was a republican warning about how foreign attachments, resentments, and passions distort judgment.

---

[40] George Washington, "Farewell Address," 1796. Washington warned that a nation indulging "habitual hatred" or "habitual fondness" toward another becomes "in some degree a slave," and may be driven into war contrary to sound policy.

The same address contains his famous advice to "steer clear of permanent alliances," while still observing existing engagements "in their genuine sense" and trusting, where necessary, to "temporary alliances for extraordinary emergencies."[41] The sentence is often quoted loosely, but in context it confirms the same disciplined posture that marked the proclamation of 1793. Washington was not preaching passivity. He was insisting that the nation preserve independence of judgment, retain freedom of choice, and avoid the sort of durable political attachment that would hand its war decisions over to foreign quarrels.

Most revealing of all, Washington explicitly tied his Farewell back to 1793. The proclamation of April 22, he wrote, was "the index of my plan." After deliberate examination, he had concluded that the United States "had a right to take, and was bound in duty and interest to take, a neutral position." Having taken it, he was determined to maintain it "with moderation, perseverance, and firmness."[42] That sentence captures the spirit of the whole chapter. Peace was not, for Washington, a mood or a passivity. It was a policy requiring discipline.

That is why Washington belongs at the beginning of any serious history of American war powers. He did not settle every future dispute, and he certainly did not prevent later executives from arguing for broader powers than he used. But he established the first great precedent. The executive might speak and act with energy in order to preserve peace, enforce the laws of neutrality, and protect the nation from being dragged by

---

41  bid. Washington wrote that it was the nation's "true policy to steer clear of permanent alliances," though existing engagements should be observed in their genuine sense and "temporary alliances" might be proper in extraordinary emergencies."

42  Ibid. Washington also wrote that his proclamation of April 22, 1793, was "the index of my plan," and that he had determined to maintain the neutral position "with moderation, perseverance, and firmness."

private citizens or foreign agents into war. What he did not establish was a presidential prerogative to place the republic into war by his own will.

The distinction was not dramatic, but it was foundational.

Washington's example also reveals something larger about republican government. Peace is not maintained by inertia alone. It requires steadiness against faction, resistance to foreign manipulation, and the willingness to let law stand between national passion and national action. In that sense, Washington's first major contribution to the American practice of war power was not a war precedent at all. It was a precedent of executive restraint in the service of peace.

The theory had been drawn in Philadelphia. Washington showed what it looked like in practice.

# Chapter 5:
# Jefferson and the Line of Defense

Washington had shown that executive energy could preserve peace without absorbing the decision for war. Jefferson's moment came under harder conditions. He did not face a diplomatic crisis alone, but a declared war and an immediate threat to American commerce. The constitutional question was therefore sharper: once hostilities had begun, how far could the President go on his own authority, and where did defense end and offense begin?

No early President was less likely to be mistaken for a passive magistrate than Jefferson. He had little taste for tribute, little patience for maritime extortion, and no desire to leave American commerce exposed to humiliation. Yet when Tripoli forced the issue in 1801, he did not claim a general executive power to carry war where he chose. Instead he drew one of the clearest constitutional lines in the early republic.

Tripoli, as Jefferson told Congress, had come forward with demands "unfounded either in right or in compact," had declared that would follow if those demands were not met, and had already put cruisers to sea. Jefferson responded by sending "a small squadron of frigates into the Mediterranean," with assurances of America's desire to remain at peace, but "with orders to protect our commerce against the threatened attack."[43]

---

[43] Thomas Jefferson, *First Annual Message to Congress*, Dec. 8, 1801. Jefferson reported that Tripoli had made demands "unfounded either in right or in compact," had declared that war would follow if those demands were not met, and that he had sent a small squadron "to protect our commerce against the threatened attack." See also Office of the Historian, U.S.

The distinction was not verbal subtlety. It was policy, and it was constitutional policy.

Jefferson then stated the principle in language that deserves to be remembered as long as the American debate over war powers endures. After the American schooner *Enterprise* had defeated and captured a Tripolitan corsair, the captured vessel was released. Why? Jefferson explained: he was "unauthorised by the constitution, without the sanction of Congress, to go beyond the line of defence." He then added that Congress might consider whether, "by authorising measures of offence also," it would place American force on an equal footing with its adversary; and he expressly referred the "important function" to the legislature, where the Constitution had "confided" it "exclusively."[44]

That passage is one of the most revealing executive statements in the constitutional history of war power. Jefferson did not deny that the President could act with speed when attack had already begun. He did deny that such defense carried with it a general right to choose the larger scope of the war. The Commander in Chief might resist, protect, and repel. He was not thereby free to enlarge the conflict into offensive operations of his own choosing.

This was not a convenient doctrine. Indeed, its very awkwardness is part of its significance. It is one thing to speak in principle of a line between defense and offense. It is another to hold that line when an enemy vessel has been beaten in action

---

Department of State, "Barbary Wars, 1801–1805 and 1815–1816," on Tripoli's tribute demand and declaration of war in 1801.

[44] Jefferson, *First Annual Message to Congress*, Dec. 8, 1801. The message states that he was "unauthorised by the constitution, without the sanction of Congress, to go beyond the line of defence," and asks whether Congress, "by authorising measures of offence also," will place American force on an equal footing with its adversary; Jefferson then refers the "important function" to the legislature exclusively.

and a victory is at hand. Jefferson's decision to release the disabled corsair, rather than convert a defensive success into a wider executive war, showed that he meant the distinction seriously. The limit was not an afterthought. It was a constitutional scruple.

Contemporaries noticed the awkwardness at once. Hamilton, writing soon afterward, mocked what he took to be the absurdity of the position. He pointed out that Jefferson's doctrine appeared to allow public force to destroy life in combat, yet not to restrain liberty or seize property afterward; in the very case of the Tripolitan vessel, men had been killed but the captured cruiser had been set free.[45] Hamilton's criticism was not frivolous. It exposed the practical strain built into Jefferson's line. A constitutional limit may be clear in theory and difficult in operation.

Yet that practical difficulty is precisely what gives Jefferson's position its weight. Had the line been easy, it would have proved little. The value of the episode lies in the fact that Jefferson refused to make convenience the measure of constitutional authority. He did not say: the enemy has declared war, therefore all force is now executive force. He said, in substance: attack may be resisted at once, but the move from defense to offense must pass through Congress.

Congress answered him in February 1802. It did not issue a formal declaration of war. Instead it enacted a statute "for the protection of the Commerce and Seamen of the United States, against the Tripolitan Cruisers." The act authorized the President to employ such armed vessels as he judged requisite for protecting American commerce and seamen, to instruct

---

[45] Alexander Hamilton, *The Examination Number I* [17 Dec. 1801]. Hamilton criticized the doctrine in the message as allowing public force to destroy life in combat while not seizing enemy liberty or property, pointing specifically to the released Tripolitan corsair.

commanders "to subdue, seize and make prize" of Tripolitan vessels and goods, and to cause such "acts of precaution or hostility" as the state of war would justify. It also authorized the President to grant "special commissions" to private armed vessels — in effect, to bring licensed private force into the conflict under national authority.[46]

This statute matters for two reasons. First, it confirms Jefferson's own constitutional understanding. Once he wanted authority to go beyond defense, he asked Congress for it. Congress then gave it, not by vague acquiescence, but by affirmative law. Second, it reveals an early American practice that would become increasingly important later: the use of statutory authorization short of a formal declaration of war. The republic did not move from peace to offensive action solely through declaration or solely through presidential initiative. It moved, in this case, through an executive defensive response followed by legislative authorization.

The inclusion of special commissions to private armed vessels is especially revealing. The constitutional power to grant letters of marque and reprisal, which can seem like a relic to modern readers, was still a living part of the founders' world. Jefferson's Mediterranean crisis therefore provides an early example of both public naval force and delegated private force passing through legislative sanction rather than executive prerogative alone.[47]

Once Congress had acted, the war naturally widened. The conflict with Tripoli continued until 1805, when the United

---

[46]  *An Act for the protection of the Commerce and Seamen of the United States, against the Tripolitan Cruisers,* Feb. 6, 1802, 2 Stat. 129, secs. 1–3. The act authorized the President to employ armed vessels for protection of commerce, to direct commanders to "subdue, seize and make prize" of Tripolitan vessels and effects, to undertake "acts of precaution or hostility," and to issue "special commissions" to private armed vessels.

[47]  Ibid.

States secured peace without any provision for continuing tribute, though ransom was paid for American prisoners. [48] The military story has its own interest. For the constitutional history of war power, however, the opening moment remains the most instructive.

Jefferson did not begin with a theory of broad executive war-making. He began with defense, drew the line there explicitly, and asked Congress to decide whether the nation would go farther. Congress answered by authorizing measures of offense, thereby transforming a defensive posture into a broader conflict under legislative sanction.

The line Jefferson described was not perfectly self-enforcing. Hamilton's criticism exposed how difficult it could be to maintain in practice, and Congress's statute showed how quickly defensive action might widen once authorization was granted. Yet these complications do not diminish the importance of Jefferson's position. In the first overseas conflict of the constitutional era, he insisted that the executive might repel attack, but that the decision to go beyond the "line of defence" belonged to Congress.

That principle would not always govern later practice. But in Jefferson's hands it remained clear.

---

[48] Office of the Historian, U.S. Department of State, "Barbary Wars, 1801–1805 and 1815–1816." The U.S. treaty with Tripoli concluded in 1805 included ransom for American prisoners but no provision for continuing tribute.

# Chapter 6:
## Jackson and the Executive
## Facts on the Ground

Jefferson had drawn the line with unusual clarity. The executive might repel attack, but could not go beyond "the line of defense" without legislative sanction. The next great test of that principle did not come from a cautious magistrate trying to hold the line. It came from a general who moved faster than constitutional theory.

Andrew Jackson is often remembered as a President of iron will. Before that, he was already something just as important for the constitutional history of war power: a man who could create facts on the ground faster than civilian government could comfortably absorb them. In the Florida campaign of 1818, the issue was not simply whether force was justified. It was whether executive initiative, once set in motion, could outrun the narrow authority under which it had been launched and force the government to choose between disavowal and ratification.

The setting was unstable from the start. Spanish authority in Florida had grown weak, Seminole raids and cross-border violence troubled the southern frontier, and American officials believed that Spain had failed in its treaty obligation to restrain hostilities from its side of the line. Monroe's administration adopted the same broad premise Jefferson had invoked in the Mediterranean: the right of self-defense did not cease at an artificial boundary when an enemy used that boundary as a shield. Yet Monroe also meant to preserve peace with Spain. In his special message of March 25, 1818, he told Congress that Jackson had been ordered not to enter Florida "unless it be in pursuit of the enemy," and, even in that case, to respect Spanish authority wherever it was maintained and to withdraw as soon as the hostile force had been reduced and frontier safety secured.[49]

That was still Jefferson's line in another form. Defensive pursuit might be necessary. War with Spain was another matter.

Monroe made the constitutional limit even plainer in private. In a July 19, 1818 letter to Jackson, he explained that occupation of Spanish posts or the taking of the province would "authorize war," and that by the principles of the Constitution the Executive was "incompetent" to take such a step. "Congress alone possess the Power."[50] Few presidential statements state the point more bluntly. The administration was prepared to justify pursuit. It was not prepared, at least in theory, to let an executive officer change the nation's relations with Spain on his own authority.

Jackson did not hold to that narrow line. In the spring of 1818 he entered Florida, destroyed Seminole villages, seized St. Marks, advanced westward, took Pensacola, and effectively occupied the principal Spanish posts implicated in the campaign. He also ordered the trial and execution of the British subjects Alexander Arbuthnot and Robert Ambrister, whom he regarded as instigators or supporters of the hostile combination against the United States.[51] However one judges the military case, the

---

[49] James Monroe, "Special Message," March 25, 1818. Monroe told Congress that Jackson was ordered not to enter Florida "unless it be in pursuit of the enemy," and in that case to respect Spanish authority wherever maintained and withdraw once the hostile tribe had been reduced and the frontier secured.

[50] James Monroe to Andrew Jackson, July 19, 1818. Monroe wrote that further occupation "would authorize war," to which "by the principles of our constitution, the Executive is incompetent. Congress alone possess the Power."

[51] Office of the Historian, U.S. Department of State, "Acquisition of Florida: Treaty of Adams-Onís (1819) and Transcontinental Treaty (1821)," noting Jackson's seizure of St. Marks and Pensacola and the execution of two

constitutional fact is plain: Jackson had moved well beyond a limited pursuit of raiders in the woods. He had done what Monroe had privately warned would amount to war if adopted as policy.

This is the point at which the chapter's title matters. Jackson created an executive fact on the ground. By the time Washington could deliberate fully, the forts had been taken, the executions carried out, the campaign celebrated by many Americans, and the question was no longer what authority should have permitted. The question was what civilian government could now do with what had already happened.

Monroe's own language shows how serious the problem was. Writing to Jefferson on July 22, 1818, he admitted that the affair at Pensacola had been "full of difficulty," and added that the administration had tried to turn it to the country's advantage "without incurring the charge of committing a breach of the Constitution, or of giving to Spain just cause of war."[52] That sentence reveals the whole predicament. The administration did not regard the issue as one of diplomacy alone. It was also a constitutional problem. If it openly adopted Jackson's actions as its own, it risked conceding that the Executive had effectively made war against Spain.

John Quincy Adams, serving as Secretary of State, answered the foreign-policy side of that dilemma with great force. He defended Jackson against Spanish and British protest, argued that Spain had failed to govern Florida or restrain the hostile forces operating there, and turned the campaign into a

---

British citizens; see also Florida Memory's summary of the First Seminole War.

[52] James Monroe to Thomas Jefferson, July 22, 1818. Monroe wrote that the "occurrence at Pensacola" had been "full of difficulty," and that the administration had tried to turn it to the country's advantage "without incurring the charge of committing a breach of the Constitution, or of giving to Spain just cause of war."

diplomatic lever. As the State Department's own historical summary puts it, Adams used Jackson's military action to present Spain with a choice: either control the inhabitants of East Florida or cede the territory to the United States.[53] This was brilliant statecraft, but it did not erase the constitutional difficulty. It converted the difficulty into advantage.

Monroe's public position, stated in his annual message of November 16, 1818, was an effort to preserve both the diplomatic gain and the constitutional line. He defended the pursuit of the Seminoles into Florida, and even acknowledged that Jackson had been "justifiable" in entering St. Marks and Pensacola because of the misconduct of Spanish officers there. Yet he immediately added that "the amicable relations existing between the United States and Spain could not be altered by that act alone." By ordering the restitution of the posts, he said, those relations were preserved. "To a change of them the power of the Executive is deemed incompetent; it is vested in Congress only."[54]

This is one of the most revealing presidential statements in the whole history of American war powers. Monroe did not deny that Jackson's military logic had force. He did not deny that Spanish weakness and Spanish misconduct had created a dangerous situation. He did not deny that the United States might rightfully defend itself in Florida. What he denied was that an executive officer's action, however successful, could by itself

---

[53] Office of the Historian, U.S. Department of State, "Acquisition of Florida: Treaty of Adams-Onís (1819) and Transcontinental Treaty (1821)." The summary states that Adams used Jackson's military action to demand that Spain either control East Florida or cede it to the United States.

[54] James Monroe, "Second Annual Message," November 16, 1818. Monroe defended the pursuit into Florida and even Jackson's entry into St. Marks and Pensacola, but insisted that "the amicable relations existing between the United States and Spain could not be altered by that act alone," and that "the power of the Executive is deemed incompetent; it is vested in Congress only."

alter the nation's political relation to Spain. That remained a congressional power.

In principle, then, Monroe reaffirmed Jefferson's line. In practice, he had been forced to draw it only after Jackson had crossed it.

That distinction matters. Jefferson held the constitutional boundary in advance and asked Congress to authorize offense before the war widened. Monroe accepted the widened reality first, then restored the constitutional boundary by insisting that the captured posts be returned and that the nation's formal relations with Spain had not changed. The two episodes are related, but not identical. Jefferson's was a model of prior restraint. Monroe's was a salvage operation after executive initiative had outrun instruction.

Yet Monroe's position was not empty. By refusing to let Jackson's military success automatically become national policy toward Spain, he preserved the constitutional principle that war, in the political sense, could not be made by executive fait accompli alone. Spain's cession of Florida in the Adams-Onís Treaty of 1819 followed not from Jackson's conquest by itself, but from subsequent diplomacy and formal agreement.[55] The treaty, concluded on February 22, 1819, transferred East and West Florida to the United States and settled broader boundary questions between the two countries.[56] The territorial result was large; the constitutional method by which the result was ultimately regularized still mattered.

That is why this episode occupies such an important place in the story of American war powers. It does not fit a simple

---

55 Office of the Historian, U.S. Department of State, "Acquisition of Florida: Treaty of Adams-Onís (1819) and Transcontinental Treaty (1821)."

56 "Treaty of Amity, Settlement, and Limits Between the United States of America, and His Catholic Majesty," signed February 22, 1819, commonly called the Adams-Onís Treaty.

lesson. It is not a clean precedent for executive war-making, because Monroe expressly denied that the Executive could alter relations with Spain on his own. It is not a clean vindication of legislative supremacy either, because Jackson's unauthorized or overextended action created the diplomatic and political situation to which the government then had to respond. The republic did not choose war in the ordinary way. It was presented with an accomplished military situation and then compelled to decide how far to own it.

This pattern would recur in later American history. Executive force would move first, sometimes under broad necessity, sometimes under ambiguous instruction, sometimes beyond the political comfort of those who had set it in motion. Civilian government would then face the harder question: whether to disavow the deed, contain it, legalize it, or convert it into advantage. Jackson's Florida campaign is one of the earliest and clearest examples of that dynamic.

The constitutional lesson is therefore not that theory failed. It is that theory met a harder adversary than paper: success. Military success creates its own pressure for ratification. Once a fort is taken, an enemy scattered, or territory occupied, statesmen find it difficult to restore the status quo simply in the name of constitutional neatness. Jackson understood that instinctively. Monroe and Adams had to govern in its wake.

Still, Monroe's public conclusion should not be forgotten. Even while exploiting the strategic gain, he insisted on the principle that the Executive was incompetent to change the nation's formal relations with Spain. Congress only could do that. In this respect the administration still spoke the language of the Constitution, even while struggling with the consequences of an officer who had outrun it.

That struggle is the real meaning of the episode. Jackson showed how easily executive initiative could create facts on the ground. Monroe showed how difficult it was to preserve constitutional boundaries once those facts had been created. Between them, they revealed a recurring truth of republican government: the most dangerous constitutional precedents are often born not from open theory, but from successful action taken too far.

# Chapter 7:
# Lincoln and the Emergency Constitution

Jackson had shown how executive initiative could create facts on the ground faster than constitutional theory could comfortably absorb them. Lincoln confronted something more severe. He did not face an unauthorized success on the frontier or an overbold subordinate, but a rebellion that threatened the life of the government itself. The constitutional question was therefore no longer whether executive energy might outrun theory in a particular campaign. It was whether constitutional government could preserve itself only by taking measures whose legality was, at best, uncertain in advance.

No American President ever confronted that question under greater pressure.

Between the fall of Fort Sumter in April 1861 and the meeting of Congress on July 4, Lincoln acted on his own authority in ways of lasting constitutional consequence. He called out the militia, enlarged the Army and Navy, proclaimed a blockade of Southern ports, spent funds without prior appropriation, and authorized a qualified suspension of the privilege of habeas corpus in places where military necessity seemed to require it.[57] In ordinary times, several of these acts would have provoked immediate constitutional objection. Lincoln did not deny that objection. He acknowledged it and answered it in the only way he thought the emergency permitted:

---

[57]  Abraham Lincoln, Special Message to Congress, July 4, 1861; see also Civil War, War Powers, and The Prize Cases, Constitution Annotated, noting Lincoln's early proclamations and Congress's later legislation recognizing them.

by arguing that the survival of the government was itself the first constitutional necessity.

That is why his July 4, 1861 message to Congress is one of the central documents in the history of American war powers. It is more than a message asking for men and money. It is Lincoln's fullest argument that extraordinary executive action may be justified when the constitutional order is under mortal attack and Congress cannot act in time. He did not claim that the Constitution disappears in emergency. He claimed that the Constitution must be read in such a way that the government it creates is not required to commit suicide out of fidelity to form.

His most famous formulation came in the habeas corpus discussion. "The whole of the laws which were required to be faithfully executed," he wrote, were "being resisted, and failing of execution, in nearly one-third of the States." He then posed the question in the starkest possible terms: "Are all the laws but one to go unexecuted, and the Government itself go to pieces, lest that one be violated?"[58] This was the language of necessity, but not of mere convenience. Lincoln was not saying that executive power expands whenever difficulties arise. He was saying that rebellion had created a situation in which insistence on ordinary process might mean the destruction of the whole constitutional system.

The force of that claim should not be understated. Jefferson had drawn a boundary between defense and offense. Monroe had insisted that the Executive was incompetent to alter the nation's formal relation to Spain. Lincoln did something more radical. He argued that certain constitutional and statutory limits might need to be bent, or at least interpreted elastically, in order

---

[58] Lincoln, Special Message to Congress, July 4, 1861. "Are all the laws but one to go unexecuted, and the Government itself go to pieces, lest that one be violated?"

to preserve the government to which those limits belonged. This was not Jackson's fact on the ground. It was an emergency theory of constitutional self-preservation.

The argument first came into open judicial conflict in *Ex parte Merryman*. After Lincoln authorized suspension of the writ along the military line between Philadelphia and Washington, Chief Justice Roger B. Taney, sitting as a circuit judge, held that the power to suspend the privilege of habeas corpus belonged to Congress, not the President.[59] Taney's position was structurally simple and powerful. The Suspension Clause appears in Article I, and therefore the power, if it exists at all, is legislative. Lincoln did not obey him. Instead, in the July 4 message, he replied indirectly that the Constitution was silent as to which branch should exercise the power, and that the provision had plainly been made for a dangerous emergency in which the danger could not be left to "run its course until Congress could be called together."[60]

This is one of the purest constitutional collisions in American history: judicial formal location of a power in Article I against executive necessity grounded in the need to keep the government alive long enough for Congress to act. Lincoln did not answer Taney with theory alone. He answered him with time. Congress did meet, and when it did, it moved in his direction. In July and August 1861 it passed legislation authorizing the President to declare certain states in insurrection and "approved and in all respects legalized" his earlier proclamations and orders

---

[59] *Ex parte Merryman*, 17 F. Cas. 144 (C.C.D. Md. 1861). For the contemporary printed text, see Henry Dutton, *Writ of Habeas Corpus. Ex-parte Merryman* (Philadelphia, 1861), Library of Congress.

[60] Lincoln, *Special Message to Congress*, July 4, 1861. Lincoln argued that the Constitution was silent as to which branch should exercise the suspension power and that the emergency could not be left to run its course until Congress assembled.

respecting the rebellion.[61] The point is important. Lincoln did not simply seize permanent emergency authority and declare the matter closed. He acted first under pressure, then sought legislative ratification after the fact.

That pattern repeated itself throughout the war. Lincoln often moved before Congress, but he also repeatedly drew Congress back into the legal structure of the emergency. This is what makes the Civil War episode more complicated than later myths allow. Lincoln did not behave as though Congress were irrelevant. He behaved as though Congress could not always act first, but must be brought in as soon as it could.

The Supreme Court's decision in *The Prize Cases* gave Lincoln's wartime theory its most famous judicial vindication. The question was whether the President could lawfully order and enforce a blockade of Southern ports before Congress had formally ratified his actions. The Court answered yes. It held that while the President "has no power to initiate or declare a war," if war is thrust upon the country by invasion or rebellion, he is "not only authorized but bound to resist force by force."[62] The Court went further still. Whether the President, in suppressing an insurrection, had encountered a civil war of such proportions as to require treating the insurgents as belligerents, it said, was a question "to be decided by him."[63]

That language did not erase the Constitution's distribution of powers, but it did stretch the executive side of it as far as

---

[61] Act of July 13, 1861, § 5, 12 Stat. 257; Act of Aug. 6, 1861, § 3, 12 Stat. 326; see also *Civil War, War Powers, and The Prize Cases, Constitution Annotated,* noting that Congress "approved and in all respects legalized" Lincoln's proclamations and orders.

[62] *The Prize Cases,* 67 U.S. (2 Black) 635, 668 (1863). The Court said the President "has no power to initiate or declare a war," but if war is forced upon the nation he is "bound to resist force by force."

[63] *The Prize Cases,* 67 U.S. (2 Black) 635, 670 (1863). Whether a civil war of such proportions existed as to require recognition of belligerency was, the Court said, a question "to be decided by him."

emergency would carry. The Court did not say Lincoln could make war as policy. It said he must meet war as fact when war had already arisen in the world. In that sense, *The Prize Cases* preserved the old theoretical line while allowing the executive broad room to act once the line had been crossed by rebellion. If Jefferson had defined the President's right to repel, the Court now gave Lincoln the authority to do far more than merely parry a blow. He could blockade, seize, and conduct the hostilities necessary to suppress a civil war already in being.

The most far-reaching of Lincoln's wartime acts came in the Emancipation Proclamation of January 1, 1863. Here again Lincoln did not rest his authority on a general legislative power or on a moral claim alone. He grounded it expressly in the war power: "by virtue of the power in me vested as Commander-in-Chief," and "as a fit and necessary war measure for suppressing said rebellion."[64] The words matter. Emancipation, in the form Lincoln gave it, was justified as emergency constitutional action tied to military necessity. He did not claim to abolish slavery everywhere by simple presidential fiat. He limited the proclamation to areas in rebellion and treated it as a weapon of war.

That move transformed the conflict. It enlarged the purposes of the war and altered the constitutional character of executive action within it. Yet it also remained recognizably part of Lincoln's emergency theory. If the rebellion threatened the nation's life, then measures necessary to suppress it might properly extend beyond the narrow battlefield and into the social order sustaining the rebellion itself. One may admire or criticize the doctrine, but one cannot deny its coherence.

---

[64] Abraham Lincoln, Emancipation Proclamation, Jan. 1, 1863. Lincoln justified the measure as one taken "by virtue of the power in me vested as Commander-in-Chief" and "as a fit and necessary war measure for suppressing said rebellion."

Still, the Civil War did not permanently constitutionalize emergency. That is one reason Lincoln's case remains so difficult and so instructive. His arguments were made under conditions of rebellion, and his strongest claims were strongest because the facts were so extreme. After the war, the Court in *Ex parte Milligan* reasserted the older limits. "The Constitution of the United States," it said, "is a law for rulers and people, equally in war and in peace." It rejected the idea that constitutional guarantees may simply be suspended by necessity whenever government finds them inconvenient.[65] Most famously, the Court declared: "Martial rule can never exist where the courts are open and in the proper and unobstructed exercise of their jurisdiction."[66]

That was not a repudiation of every wartime measure Lincoln had taken. It was a warning against allowing emergency to become ordinary rule. The Court conceded that in actual theaters of war, where courts were closed and civil authority displaced, martial rule might be necessary. But it refused to let the war dissolve the distinction between emergency necessity and normal constitutional life. In Indiana, where the courts were open, military trials of civilians could not stand.[67]

The relationship between Lincoln and *Milligan* is therefore more subtle than simple opposition suggests. Lincoln had argued that government must not be allowed to perish because law cannot be perfectly kept in rebellion. *Milligan* answered that government need not and must not preserve itself by converting

---

[65] *Ex parte Milligan*, 71 U.S. (4 Wall.) 2, 120–21 (1866). "The Constitution of the United States is a law for rulers and people, equally in war and in peace."

[66] *Ex parte Milligan*, 71 U.S. (4 Wall.) 2, 127 (1866). "Martial rule can never exist where the courts are open and in the proper and unobstructed exercise of their jurisdiction." See also the Court's statement that martial law cannot arise from a merely threatened invasion.

[67] Ibid.

emergency into permanent doctrine where ordinary law can still operate. Put differently, Lincoln stated the strongest case for emergency executive power in American history; *Milligan* stated one of the strongest postwar correctives.

That tension is the real subject of this chapter.

Lincoln did not just enlarge executive power. He articulated an emergency constitution: an understanding under which certain extraordinary measures could be justified because the alternative was national collapse. Yet he also sought congressional ratification, held elections, and continued to speak the language of constitutional government rather than naked necessity. He was not a Caesar claiming a superior title to rule. He was a President claiming that the Constitution, if it is to remain more than parchment, cannot require the government to die in order to keep every form intact at every moment of rebellion.

That claim carried terrible risks, and Lincoln knew it. So does any reader of the later American history of emergency power. Once necessity is admitted as constitutional argument, later executives may invoke it in circumstances far less grave than civil war. That is why Lincoln's case cannot be treated either as a simple vindication or as a simple warning. It is both.

He showed the strongest reason a republic may ever have for enlarging executive action: survival. He also showed the danger of leaving that enlargement without later correction, ratification, or judicial limit. In that sense, Lincoln is the high-water mark of the emergency constitution — not because he destroyed the Constitution, but because he forced it to answer the hardest question any republic can face: whether law can preserve itself when the life of the state is at stake.

# Part III:
# The Drift Begins

# Chapter 8:
## The Last Declarations

Before declarations disappeared from American practice, they passed through one final constitutional age. That age included two world wars, not one. The first showed the older form under pressure. The second gave it its last full expression. They were the last great declarations, the last major wars in which the republic entered conflict through the older and more formal constitutional grammar before the language of authorization began to replace the language of declaration.[68]

*World War I: The Old Form Under Strain*

The United States did not enter the First World War in a rush of unanimity. It entered after years of neutrality, argument, and increasing strain. When war broke out in Europe in 1914, Wilson declared America's intention to remain neutral and urged Americans to remain impartial "in thought as well as deed." Yet neutrality grew harder to maintain as the conflict widened, American commerce became entangled with the Allied cause, German submarine warfare intensified, and public feeling divided sharply over what neutrality required and what national honor would permit.[69]

---

[68] U.S. Senate Historical Office, "About Declarations of War by Congress," stating that Congress approved its last formal declaration of war during World War II.

[69] National Archives, "Joint Address to Congress Leading to a Declaration of War Against Germany (1917)." The Archives notes Wilson's original neutrality posture in 1914.

What makes 1917 so important constitutionally is not only that the pressures were immense, but that Wilson still refused to treat those pressures as a warrant for executive war-making. In his war message of April 2, 1917, he told Congress that the choices before the nation were "very serious" and that it was "neither right nor constitutionally permissible" for him to assume the responsibility of making them alone. He also acknowledged that he had previously hoped "armed neutrality" might suffice, but now judged it "impracticable."[70] In other words, even after years of mounting crisis, Wilson did not claim that the President could carry the republic from peace into war by executive determination. He asked Congress for a declaration.

Congress answered in the older form. On April 6, 1917, the United States formally declared war on Germany. The Senate had approved the resolution 82–6; the House did so by 373–50. Later that year, on December 7, Congress declared war on Austria-Hungary as well, the Senate voting 74–0.[71] The constitutional mechanism remained intact. However difficult the nation's neutrality had become, however far preparation and executive diplomacy had already moved the country toward belligerency, the final legal step from peace into war still passed through declaration.

The burden of the war was also still national and visible. The Selective Service System records 2,810,296 inductions during

---

[70] National Archives, "Joint Address to Congress Leading to a Declaration of War Against Germany (1917)." The Archives notes Wilson's original neutrality posture in 1914 and the increasing difficulty of maintaining it; Wilson's April 2, 1917 message states that the decision before the nation was "neither right nor constitutionally permissible" for him to make alone, and that "armed neutrality" had proved "impracticable."

[71] U.S. Senate, "Declaration of War with Germany, WWI (S.J.Res. 1)," giving the Senate vote of 82–6; U.S. House of Representatives, "The House Declaration of War Against Germany in 1917," giving the House vote of 373–50; and U.S. Senate, "Declaration of War with Austria-Hungary, WWI (H.J.Res. 169)," giving the Senate vote of 74–0.

World War I.[72] That figure matters for more than military accounting. It means that the conflict, once declared, did not rest on a narrow professional force alone. The republic still imposed the burden broadly enough that war remained a fact of civic life, beyond executive policy.

This is why World War I belongs in this chapter. It does not mark the abandonment of the old constitutional form. It marks the old form under strain. Neutrality was contested, executive preparation and diplomatic positioning mattered enormously, and the road to war was neither simple nor politically unanimous. Yet the republic still crossed the final threshold through Congress. The declaration was not a decorative afterthought. It remained the constitutional act by which war was made public, lawful, and national.

## World War II: The Final Alignment

If World War I showed the old form under pressure, World War II showed it in its last and clearest alignment. No later American conflict would bring together so completely the elements the founders would most readily have associated with war in a republic: direct attack, overwhelming public assent, formal declaration, mass mobilization, and broadly shared burden.[73]

The sequence began with Pearl Harbor. On the morning of December 7, 1941, Japanese forces launched a surprise attack on American military and naval installations in Hawaii. The

---

[72] Selective Service System, "Induction Statistics," recording 2,810,296 World War I inductions.

[73] U.S. Senate Historical Office, "About Declarations of War by Congress," stating that Congress approved its last formal declaration of war during World War II and listing the declaration votes for Germany in 1917, Austria-Hungary in 1917, Japan in 1941, Germany in 1941, Italy in 1941, and Bulgaria, Hungary, and Rumania in 1942.

National Archives records 3,435 casualties, together with catastrophic losses in ships and aircraft.[74] Whatever room there had been in earlier controversies for argument over whether war had effectively begun, Pearl Harbor left very little. The attack was not a diplomatic pressure or a frontier emergency. It was war forced upon the United States in an unmistakable and public form.

Roosevelt's address to Congress the next day therefore stands as one of the clearest constitutional moments in American history. He did not simply announce retaliation or assume the nation's belligerent status on his own authority. He asked Congress to declare that a state of war existed between the United States and Japan.[75] Congress complied at once. The Senate voted 82–0, and the House 388–1, with Jeannette Rankin casting the lone dissenting vote.[76] Three days later, after Germany and Italy declared war on the United States, Congress responded with formal declarations against both as well; the Senate voted 88–0 against Germany and 90–0 against Italy.[77] In June 1942, Congress formally declared war on Bulgaria, Hungary, and Rumania.[78]

This was the older constitutional grammar in full. Congress declared war. As the Senate Historical Office notes, Congress

---

[74] National Archives, "Attack on Pearl Harbor," recording 3,435 casualties.

[75] National Archives, National Archives, "Joint Address to Congress Leading to a Declaration of War Against Japan," on Roosevelt's request for a declaration.

[76] U.S. House of Representatives, "The Declaration of War Against Japan," and House tally-sheet material recording the House's 388–1 vote; the Senate's vote was 82–0. The rationale for Representative Rankin's dissenting vote was expressed on the floor: "As a woman I can't go to war, and I refuse to send anyone else."

[77] U.S. Senate Historical Office, "About Declarations of War by Congress," listing 1941 declaration votes for Germany and Italy.

[78] U.S. Senate Historical Office, "About Declarations of War by Congress," listing 1942 declaration votes for Bulgaria, Hungary, and Rumania.

approved its last formal declaration of war during World War II.[79] After that, the declarations ceased.

The civic burden of the war matched its constitutional form. Before Pearl Harbor, Congress had already enacted the Selective Training and Service Act of September 16, 1940, the nation's first peacetime draft law. By the end of the war, over 45 million men had been registered, 15 million had served, approximately 66 percent of those who served had been inducted, and the total number inducted was 10,110,104.[80] These figures are not merely military statistics. They describe the social character of the conflict. World War II was not fought by a narrow professional force insulated from the ordinary citizen. Its burden was distributed broadly enough that the nation unmistakably knew itself to be at war.

That is why World War II remains the constitutional benchmark. The law, the political act, and the civic burden all pointed in the same direction. Congress declared war; the President commanded the forces once war existed; and the people bore the cost openly and at scale. Later conflicts would still involve congressional support and executive command, but the alignment of declaration, assent, and shared burden would never again appear so completely.

---

[79] U.S. Senate Historical Office, "About Declarations of War by Congress," stating that Congress approved its last formal declaration of war during World War II.

[80] Selective Service System, "Historical Timeline," stating that the Selective Training and Service Act of September 16, 1940 was the nation's first peacetime draft law, and that by the end of the war over 45 million men had been registered, 15 million had served, approximately 66 percent were inducted, and the total number inducted was 10,110,104.

# Chapter 9:
## Korea and the Eclipse of Declaration

Korea was not the first great American war. It was the first great American war after the declaration had vanished.

That sentence marks a hinge in constitutional history. With Korea, the older grammar of war power did not disappear all at once, but it ceased to govern the nation's entry into major conflict. The United States would still fight with armies, fleets, appropriations, and congressional support. Citizens would still serve and die. What changed was the public legal act by which the republic openly altered its condition from peace to war. In Korea, that act was no longer a declaration.

The crisis began on June 25, 1950, when North Korean forces crossed the 38th parallel and invaded South Korea. The United Nations Security Council responded rapidly. Resolution 82 called upon the invading forces to cease hostilities and withdraw. Resolution 83 recommended that member states furnish such assistance as might be necessary to repel the attack and restore peace and security. Resolution 84, adopted on July 7, recommended a unified command under the United States and authorized the use of the United Nations flag in the operation.[81]

Truman moved just as quickly. In his statement of June 27, 1950, he announced that "in these circumstances" he had ordered United States air and sea forces "to give the Korean

---

[81] United Nations Security Council resolutions 82 (June 25, 1950), 83 (June 27, 1950), and 84 (July 7, 1950); the Security Council's 1950 resolutions list these as the Korea resolutions, and the Constitution Annotated summarizes them as authorizing the UN-based military response.

Government troops cover and support."[82] This was the decisive step. American forces entered major hostilities without a declaration of war and without prior congressional authorization under domestic law. Truman did not first ask Congress to change the nation's legal condition. He acted, and then reported.

The form of the action mattered as much as the action itself. Two days later, at a press conference, Truman agreed with a reporter who characterized the intervention as a "United Nations police action."[83] The phrase would become famous, and often notorious, because it signaled an attempt to place the conflict in a different constitutional and rhetorical category. This was not described as war in the older American sense. It was collective security, international police action, enforcement of United Nations resolutions. The label did not alter the bullets, the casualties, or the constitutional stakes. But it did alter the language in which those stakes were publicly presented.

That change in language was not incidental. It was part of the constitutional transformation. The older declaration model had involved a public legislative act by which the nation openly moved from peace into war. Korea replaced that with a different sequence: executive action first, justified in part by international authorization, followed by congressional funding and domestic support after hostilities were already underway. Congress did not disappear, but the declaration did.

Truman's Special Message to Congress of July 19, 1950 illustrates the new sequence precisely. He did not ask Congress whether the nation should enter the conflict; that decision had already been made in practice. Instead he reported what had

---

[82] Harry S. Truman, "Statement by the President on the Situation in Korea," June 27, 1950: "I have ordered United States air and sea forces to give the Korean Government troops cover and support."

[83] Harry S. Truman, "The President's News Conference," June 29, 1950, in which Truman confirmed that he meant a "United Nations police action."

been done and asked for legislation and appropriations necessary to sustain the effort.[84] Congress then extended the draft and appropriated funds, but it did not declare war and did not enact a formal authorization for the use of military force.[85] The constitutional role of the legislature had shifted from prior act to subsequent support.

This shift immediately raised objections. Senator Robert Taft questioned whether the President had legal authority to embark on what he called "a de facto war" without consulting Congress and without congressional approval.[86] The criticism went directly to the heart of the constitutional issue. If a major war could be entered by executive order under the umbrella of a Security Council resolution, then the Declare War Clause had not been abolished, but it had been bypassed.

The Truman administration answered with a legal theory as consequential as the action itself. On July 3, 1950, the Department of State prepared a memorandum entitled *Authority of the President to Repel the Attack in Korea*. It defended the intervention as an "international police action" taken pursuant to the President's constitutional powers and the obligations of the United States under the United Nations system. More striking still, the memorandum cited a long catalog of prior

---

[84]  Harry S. Truman, "Special Message to the Congress Reporting on the Situation in Korea," July 19, 1950. Truman reported actions already taken, described the UN resolutions, and stated that the United States was determined to support the UN effort to restore peace and security in Korea.

[85]  *Constitution Annotated*, "International Police Action and the Korean War," stating that President Truman did not seek congressional authorization under domestic law, that Congress enacted neither a declaration of war nor an authorization for use of military force, and that Congress later extended the draft and appropriated funds.

[86]  *Constitution Annotated*, citing 96 Cong. Rec. 9319–23 (1950) for Senator Robert Taft's objection that the President had embarked on "a de facto war" without consulting Congress and without congressional approval.

presidential uses of force abroad — eighty-five instances — to argue that historical practice showed that express congressional permission was not constitutionally required whenever the President used military force to protect American interests.[87]

That memorandum is one of the great turning points in the practical constitutional history of war powers. Earlier American Presidents had often acted first in defense, and Congress had often ratified or legalized those actions after the fact. But Korea systematized something broader: the use of accumulated presidential precedent itself as a legal argument for large-scale hostilities. Historical practice was no longer just background. It was becoming doctrine.

Yet the transformation was not complete. Korea retained important features of the older model even as declaration disappeared. The burden of the war was still broad and plainly national. The Selective Service System records 1,529,539 inductions during the Korean War.[88] The Constitution Annotated notes that the conflict ultimately involved more than 5.7 million American military personnel and over 36,000 American casualties.[89] So although the nation no longer entered war through declaration, it still fought through mass mobilization, public sacrifice, and congressional funding. The eclipse of declaration did not yet mean the full narrowing of civic burden that would become more visible in later decades.

---

[87] U.S. Department of State, *Authority of the President to Repel the Attack in Korea* (July 3, 1950), as cited in H.R. Rep. No. 81-2495 and summarized in the *Constitution Annotated*. The memorandum defended the intervention as an "international police action" and cited eighty-five prior presidential uses of force to support executive authority.

[88] Selective Service System, "Induction Statistics," listing 1,529,539 inductions for the Korean War.

[89] *Constitution Annotated*, "International Police Action and the Korean War," The entry notes the scale of service and casualties.

This makes Korea constitutionally different from both World War II and Vietnam. It lacked the formal declaration that had defined the older model, but it did not yet display the more attenuated burden and looser political ownership of later conflicts. It stands, therefore, as an intermediate case: the first major break in constitutional form, while much of the older social and military reality still remained.

Even within the Korean War itself, executive power did not move unchecked. In 1952, when Truman attempted to seize the steel mills in order to avert a strike that might interrupt war production, the Supreme Court rejected the claim. In *Youngstown Sheet & Tube Co. v. Sawyer*, the Court held that the President could not take possession of private property without authorization from Congress or the Constitution.[90] Korea had eclipsed declaration, but it had not erased all constitutional limits. Emergency still met resistance when it moved beyond what the law had granted.

That, too, is part of the meaning of Korea. The constitutional order did not simply collapse into presidential war. Rather, the point of entry changed. Executive initiative, international authorization, and later congressional support displaced the old public act of declaration. The republic still fought; Congress still funded; the courts still sometimes pushed back. But the threshold had been altered.

This is why Korea deserves its place as the opening chapter of the drift. After 1950, the United States would repeatedly use force without formal declaration. Congress would often remain involved, sometimes heavily so, but in different ways: resolutions, appropriations, political acquiescence, later

---

[90] *Youngstown Sheet & Tube Co. v. Sawyer*, 343 U.S. 579 (1952), official U.S. Reports text via the Library of Congress. The Court rejected Truman's steel seizure during the Korean War.

authorizations. The old grammar had not been wholly erased, but it had been overshadowed by a new one.

Korea, then, is not only a war in the sequence of wars. It is the constitutional moment at which declaration ceased to be the normal doorway into major American conflict.

The manner in which the Korean War ended reinforces the same constitutional shift. Hostilities did not conclude with a treaty ratified by the Senate, as in earlier wars. Instead, they were suspended by an armistice agreement signed on July 27, 1953. The conflict ceased active fighting, but it was not legally concluded in the traditional sense. The armistice established the terms of that suspension, and over time that provisional arrangement hardened into a condition that functions as peace without the form of peace.

This absence of formal closure mirrors the absence of declaration at the outset. The republic had entered a major war without the public legislative act that once marked the transition from peace to war, and it exited without the corresponding act that traditionally restored a formal state of peace. The constitutional grammar had shifted at both ends.

Korea therefore stands not only as the point at which declaration was eclipsed, but also as the moment when the older symmetry between entry and conclusion began to dissolve. The nation fought, sustained, and ended a major conflict through new forms, while the older forms remained in the text of the Constitution but receded in practice.

# Chapter 10:
# Vietnam — Blank Check, Draft, and Disillusion

Korea had eclipsed declaration. Vietnam revealed what that eclipse could become.

The United States did not enter the Vietnam War by formal declaration. It entered through a congressional resolution passed in haste, framed in general terms, and later stretched far beyond the circumstances that had produced it. In early August 1964, after two reported attacks on American destroyers in the Gulf of Tonkin, President Lyndon Johnson asked Congress for authority to respond. On August 7, Congress approved the Gulf of Tonkin Resolution; the Senate voted 88–2, and the House approved it unanimously. Johnson signed it on August 10. The resolution authorized the President to take "all necessary measures" to repel armed attack and prevent further aggression in Southeast Asia, and it soon became the legal basis for the Johnson and Nixon administrations' prosecution of the war.[91]

The constitutional problem lay not only in the absence of a declaration, but in the character of what replaced it. This was not

---

[91] Office of the Historian, U.S. Department of State, "U.S. Involvement in the Vietnam War: the Gulf of Tonkin and Escalation, 1964," noting that after two reported attacks in early August 1964, Johnson requested congressional authority, and that on August 7 Congress passed the Gulf of Tonkin Resolution, which authorized the President to take any measures he believed necessary and became the legal basis for the Johnson and Nixon administrations' prosecution of the war; see also U.S. Senate Historical Office, "Chairman J. William Fulbright and the 1964 Tonkin Gulf Resolution," stating that the Senate approved the resolution 88–2, the House approved it unanimously, and Johnson signed it on August 10, 1964.

a narrow authorization tied to a clearly bounded campaign. It was an enabling resolution broad enough to support years of escalation. Even at the time, Senator Wayne Morse warned that it was "a predated declaration of war." Chairman J. William Fulbright, who shepherded the measure through the Senate, admitted during debate that it gave the President authority to use force that could lead into war without further congressional declaration. The older act by which the republic openly altered its condition had not simply been omitted. It had been replaced by a resolution so elastic that later events could be fitted into it almost at will.[92]

The war that followed showed what such elasticity meant in practice. In early 1965, under the authority of the Tonkin Gulf Resolution, Johnson approved a sustained bombing campaign against North Vietnam and ordered the first U.S. combat troops into South Vietnam. By the end of 1965, more than 150,000 American combat troops had entered the country; by 1968 the number had risen above 530,000.[93] A 1968 internal memorandum later summarized the logic of the escalation with devastating precision: the history of the war since 1965, it said, had been marked by "repeated miscalculations" about the force and time required, and "each fresh increment of American power" had been justified as the last one needed to do the job.[94]

---

[92] U.S. Senate Historical Office, "Chairman J. William Fulbright and the 1964 Tonkin Gulf Resolution." The Senate history notes that Fulbright conceded the resolution gave the President authority to use force that could lead into war without a declaration, and records Wayne Morse's warning that it was "a predated declaration of war."

[93] U.S. Senate Historical Office, "Chairman J. William Fulbright and the 1964 Tonkin Gulf Resolution," noting that more than 150,000 U.S. combat troops entered South Vietnam by the end of 1965 and that the total exceeded 530,000 by 1968.

[94] Foreign Relations of the United States, 1964–1968, vol. VI, doc. 126, lines 59–60, stating that U.S. involvement since 1965 had been marked by

That is why the title of this chapter begins with the phrase *blank check*. Congress had acted, but it had acted once, broadly, and under conditions of urgency and trust. The declaration's older function — forcing the nation to confront openly the fact and scope of war — had been displaced by a resolution capable of sustaining a major conflict without requiring the republic to pass repeatedly through that same public threshold. The problem was made worse by the later controversy surrounding the alleged second Gulf of Tonkin attack of August 4, 1964. As the years passed, the sense spread that Congress had voted for war on the basis of a hurried and incomplete account, and that the administration had treated ambiguity as if it were certainty.[95]

Yet Vietnam was not limited to a constitutional problem of authorization. It was also a social and civic problem of burden. The Selective Service System records 1,857,304 inductions during the Vietnam War and notes that Selective Service provided 20 percent of the men in uniform. The same official history also notes that protest over "unfair deferments" became a major issue as anti-war sentiment deepened.[96] This matters because Vietnam was not fought by a narrow professional force

---

"repeated miscalculations" and that each fresh increment of American power had been justified as the last one needed.

[95] Office of the Historian, "U.S. Involvement in the Vietnam War: the Gulf of Tonkin and Escalation, 1964"; and NSA historical release materials on the Gulf of Tonkin. A declassified NSA study later argued that no attack occurred on the night of August 4 and that relevant SIGINT had been presented in a way that supported the contrary claim; the NSA release page itself notes that the released materials are provided for public analysis and do not represent official institutional conclusions. Later controversy over the alleged second attack contributed to the sense that Congress had acted on a hurried and incomplete record.

[96] Selective Service System, "Historical Timeline" and "Induction Statistics." The Selective Service states that it provided 20 percent of the men in uniform during the Vietnam War, that total inductions were 1,857,304, and that the draft encountered protest over "unfair deferments" fueled by anti-war sentiment.

insulated from the nation at large. The draft spread the burden widely enough to make the war a personal fact in millions of homes, campuses, and local communities, while deferment practices made that burden appear unequal and therefore unjust.

The broad burden of the war might have sustained legitimacy had the government's account of progress remained credible. Instead, it helped magnify disillusion. In late January 1968, during the Tet holiday, North Vietnamese and Viet Cong forces launched coordinated attacks across South Vietnam, including strikes in major cities and an assault on the U.S. Embassy compound in Saigon. Militarily, the offensive was eventually repelled. Politically, it did something more damaging. It weakened public support for the war by making clear that the enemy was not nearly so broken as official optimism had often implied. The Office of the Historian states the point directly: the Tet Offensive played an important role in weakening U.S. public support for the war.[97]

That weakening of support did not arise from Tet alone. By 1966 Senator Fulbright's Foreign Relations Committee had begun televised hearings on the war. Those hearings, according to the Senate's own historical account, revealed the Johnson administration's "intentional deceptions" about the war's progress and widened what came to be called the "credibility gap." Fulbright himself later confessed "a very deep moral responsibility" for having helped lead the Senate into the Tonkin

---

[97] Office of the Historian, "U.S. Involvement in the Vietnam War: The Tet Offensive, 1968," stating that North Vietnamese and Viet Cong forces launched coordinated attacks across South Vietnam in late January 1968 and that the Tet Offensive played an important role in weakening U.S. public support for the war. The same account notes that the attack on urban targets and the U.S. Embassy compound in Saigon had a powerful psychological effect.

Gulf Resolution.[98] The man who had once eased the resolution through the chamber on trust now became one of the central figures in Congress's effort to recover its judgment.

This is the constitutional significance of Vietnam. Korea had shown that a major war could be fought without declaration. Vietnam showed what could happen when a broad enabling resolution, joined to executive escalation, mass conscription, and official overstatement, carried the nation into a prolonged conflict without the old public act of war. Congress had not vanished. It had voted, funded, extended the draft, and supported the effort for years. But it had done so under a form that blurred responsibility rather than clarifying it.

The lesson is therefore not simply that Congress failed to act. It is that Congress acted in a way that no longer forced the republic to face the legal and political reality of war in the older manner. The declaration had disappeared; in its place stood a resolution broad enough to become a warrant for drift. The result was more than escalation abroad but also disillusion at home.

Korea had eclipsed declaration. Vietnam turned that eclipse into a national crisis of legitimacy.

---

[98] U.S. Senate Historical Office, "Chairman J. William Fulbright and the 1964 Tonkin Gulf Resolution," stating that televised Foreign Relations Committee hearings beginning in 1966 revealed the administration's "intentional deceptions" and widened the "credibility gap," and quoting Fulbright's later statement that he felt "a very deep moral responsibility" for having misled the Senate and the country.

# Chapter 11:
# Congress Strikes Back —
# The War Powers Resolution & the Purse

Vietnam did not teach Congress that it had no power. It taught Congress that it had used its power badly, and then used it too late.

The first step in that lesson was the repeal of the Gulf of Tonkin Resolution in 1971. Congress had finally withdrawn the broad statutory instrument by which the Johnson and Nixon administrations had justified the war, and had also called for the prompt and orderly withdrawal of American forces. Yet the bombing continued. The legal and political effect of repeal proved weaker than many had hoped. Congress could rescind an earlier blank check and still find that the war, once begun and institutionally entrenched, did not simply stop. The old declaration had disappeared; but the newer resolution, once enacted, was not easily unwound by symbolism alone.[99]

After Vietnam, Congress therefore moved on two tracks at once. It sought, first, to create a general constitutional framework for future crises; second, it used the harder and older instrument of appropriations to stop one war already in progress. The first of these efforts became famous. The second was stronger.

The War Powers Resolution of 1973 was Congress's attempt to restore what the statute itself called the "collective

---

[99] *Constitution Annotated*, ArtI.S8.C11.2.5.10, "Presidential and Congressional Power in the Vietnam War," notes that in 1971 Congress repealed the Gulf of Tonkin Resolution, that President Nixon signed the repeal measure, and that aerial campaigns nonetheless continued afterward.

judgment" of both branches in the introduction of American forces into hostilities. Its declared purpose was to fulfill the Constitution's original design and to ensure that presidential initiative in war would not drift indefinitely without legislative participation. The Resolution stated that the President's power to introduce United States forces into hostilities, or into situations where hostilities were clearly indicated, could be exercised only pursuant to a declaration of war, specific statutory authorization, or a national emergency created by attack upon the United States, its territories or possessions, or its armed forces. It further required consultation with Congress "in every possible instance" before such introduction, a report within forty-eight hours after the fact, and termination within sixty days unless Congress had declared war, specifically authorized the action, or extended the period by law. A further thirty days could be allowed for military necessity relating to safe withdrawal.[100]

That framework was ambitious, but it was also an in-between thing. It did not simply revive the old declaration model. It assumed, as a practical matter, that Presidents might act first and that Congress would then have to react under a statutory clock. At the same time, Congress was careful not to state that it was granting the President any new authority by doing so. The Resolution expressly provided that nothing in it was intended to alter the constitutional authority of Congress or the President, and that nothing in it should be construed as granting authority

---

[100] *War Powers Resolution*, Pub. L. 93-148, §§ 2–5, codified at 50 U.S.C. §§ 1541–1544. The Resolution states that its purpose is to ensure the "collective judgment" of both branches; provides in § 2(c) that presidential introduction of forces into hostilities rests on declaration, specific statutory authorization, or attack-created national emergency; requires consultation "in every possible instance" in § 3; requires a report within forty-eight hours in § 4; and establishes the sixty-day period, with a possible additional thirty days, in § 5(b).

to the President to introduce forces into hostilities.[101] That tension is the heart of the statute. The Resolution tried to restrain executive initiative without conceding that such initiative was lawful merely because the statute described what should happen after it occurred.

Nixon understood the point immediately and rejected it. In his veto message of October 24, 1973, he called the Resolution both unconstitutional and dangerous. Congress answered with unusual force. On November 7, the House overrode the veto by 284 to 135, and the Senate by 75 to 18. The statute thus became law over presidential objection, one of the clearest legislative assertions of war authority in modern American history.[102]

Yet even in victory Congress had revealed the altered terrain on which it was fighting. The War Powers Resolution was not a clean restoration of the founders' design. It was an effort to preserve that design after practice had already drifted away from it. The Resolution still presupposed executive action in advance of full legislative decision; it then sought to surround that action with consultation, reporting, and a deadline. In form, it was Congress striking back. In structure, it was Congress accommodating itself to a world in which Presidents had already learned to move first.[103]

---

[101] *War Powers Resolution*, Pub. L. 93-148, § 8(d), codified at 50 U.S.C. § 1547(d). The Resolution provides that nothing in it is intended to alter the constitutional authority of Congress or the President and that nothing in it shall be construed as granting presidential authority to introduce United States forces into hostilities.

[102] Richard Nixon, "Veto of the War Powers Resolution," October 24, 1973, calling the measure unconstitutional and dangerous; *Deschler's Precedents*, ch. 13, § 4.2, recording the November 7, 1973 override votes of 284–135 in the House and 75–18 in the Senate.

[103] *War Powers Resolution*, Pub. L. 93-148, §§ 2–5, codified at 50 U.S.C. §§ 1541–1544. The Resolution states that its purpose is to ensure the "collective judgment" of both branches; provides in § 2(c) that presidential introduction of forces into hostilities rests on declaration, specific statutory authorization, or attack-created national emergency;

The second congressional response was blunter, less elegant, and more effective. Congress used the power of the purse.

That power had always been the legislature's hardest constitutional instrument, but Vietnam made its practical meaning unmistakable. Repeals, hearings, censures, and speeches could wound a war politically. Money could stop it. In July 1973 Congress enacted a continuing appropriations measure providing that, on or after August 15, 1973, no funds therein or previously appropriated could be used to finance directly or indirectly combat activities by United States military forces in or over, or from off the shores of, North Vietnam, South Vietnam, Laos, or Cambodia. The date was fixed; the money ended; the combat role ceased.[104]

This is the moment at which Congress most clearly recovered its constitutional leverage. The legislature moved beyond protest of the war. It terminated the legal means of continuing it. For all the later fame of the War Powers Resolution, the appropriations cutoff was the harder act. It showed that if Congress truly wished to end a conflict, it possessed the power to do so in the most concrete form available to constitutional government: by refusing to pay for continued fighting.

But the bluntness of the instrument must also be noticed. The purse is powerful, yet it is often politically late. It does not

---

requires consultation "in every possible instance" in § 3; requires a report within forty-eight hours in § 4; and establishes the sixty-day period, with a possible additional thirty days, in § 5(b).

[104] Pub. L. 93-52, § 108, 87 Stat. 130 (July 1, 1973), quoted in official House precedents as providing that, on or after August 15, 1973, no funds therein or previously appropriated could be used to finance combat activities by United States military forces in or over, or from off the shores of, North Vietnam, South Vietnam, Laos, or Cambodia. See also later congressional discussion citing the same language as the 1973 Southeast Asia cutoff.

necessarily prevent the beginning of a war; it can instead force a later confrontation over whether the nation is willing to continue paying for one already underway. That was exactly the dilemma Vietnam had created. Congress had supported, enabled, funded, and extended the war for years before it finally used the only lever that could not be ignored. The purse restored authority, but it restored it at the end of a long constitutional failure.

There was another difficulty as well. One enforcement device built into the War Powers Resolution itself was unstable from the beginning. Section 5(c) purported to allow Congress to direct removal of forces by concurrent resolution.[105] But the Supreme Court's later decision in *INS v. Chadha* held that legislative veto devices are exercises of legislative power and therefore must satisfy the Constitution's requirements of bicameralism and presentment.[106] After *Chadha*, Congress could not confidently rely on a concurrent-resolution mechanism to compel withdrawal. The Resolution survived, but one of its sharpest procedural teeth was no longer secure.

That development did not destroy the statute, but it clarified the constitutional landscape. The War Powers Resolution remained important as a reporting and consultation framework and as a statement of congressional principle. The ultimate legislative sanction, however, still lay elsewhere: in ordinary

---

[105]  A concurrent resolution is a measure adopted by both houses of Congress but not presented to the President for signature or veto.

[106]  The Constitution requires that exercises of legislative power pass both houses of Congress (bicameralism) and then be presented to the President for approval or veto (presentment). See U.S. Const. art. I, §7. In *INS v. Chadha* (1983), the Supreme Court held that legislative veto mechanisms lacking presentment to the President violate these constitutional requirements. Although *Chadha* involved a one-house veto relating to executive immigration determinations, the decision cast serious doubt on the War Powers Resolution's provision allowing Congress to direct troop withdrawal by concurrent resolution without presidential presentment.

legislation, specific authorization, or appropriations. The Constitution's deepest check was not procedural cleverness. It was control of law and money.

That is why this must be viewed as more than the story of a single statute. After Vietnam, Congress struck back in two distinct ways. It wrote a framework intended to restrain presidential initiative, and it used the older and harder instrument of appropriations to end the war that had made that framework necessary. The first measure declared a constitutional principle. The second exercised a constitutional power.

The distinction matters. The War Powers Resolution is famous because it attempted to define how the war power ought to operate between the branches. The appropriations cutoff mattered because it demonstrated how Congress can actually compel an end to war when it chooses to act.

Together the two measures defined the post-Vietnam settlement. The declaration had not been restored, and the executive had not been stripped of initiative. But Congress had reasserted that war could not continue indefinitely on presidential will alone. Behind every framework, report, or resolution remained the Constitution's oldest legislative weapon: control of the purse.

# Part IV:
# The Shadow Constitution

# Chapter 12:
# Nicaragua — A Repeating Theater

Some countries enter the constitutional history of American war powers once, in one crisis, and then recede. Nicaragua does not. It returns. Again and again it appears as a place where the United States uses force, or threatens force, or organizes force through others, while speaking a language somewhat different from the old language of declared war. That is why Nicaragua belongs at the opening of Part IV. It is more than just another case. It is a recurring stage on which the same constitutional temptations reappear in changing form.

The pattern begins early. A Congressional Research Service inventory of uses of American armed force abroad lists repeated interventions in Nicaragua stretching back to the 19th century: landings in 1853, the bombardment of San Juan del Norte in 1854, further protections of "American interests" in 1896 and 1898, another landing in 1910, and then the longer interventions of 1912–1925 and 1926–1933.[107] The point is not that every one of these episodes was equal in scale or significance. The point is that Nicaragua became, for the United States, a familiar place for action below the threshold of declared war.

That familiarity did not arise by accident. Nicaragua occupied an outsized place in American strategic thought because of its location in Central America, its recurring political instability, and the long-standing attraction of canal routes and financial influence in the Caribbean basin. The State

---

[107] Congressional Research Service, *Instances of Use of United States Armed Forces Abroad, 1798–2021*, listing repeated Nicaragua interventions in 1853, 1854, 1896, 1898, 1910, 1912–1925, and 1926–1933.

Department's own summary of "Dollar Diplomacy" under Taft and Knox identifies Nicaragua as one of the clearest examples of a policy that sought to use American financial and political power to secure strategic interests while avoiding the formal costs of annexation or open war.[108] In such a setting, the United States did not need to declare war in the old sense in order to act repeatedly and forcefully. It needed only a continuing rationale of order, protection, stability, and influence.

That rationale became explicit in the crisis of 1909–1912. In December 1909, after Washington had broken relations with Nicaraguan President José Santos Zelaya, Zelaya resigned. The State Department's country summary notes that the Marines remained stationed in Nicaragua until 1932, aside from a nine-month interval in 1925–1926.[109] That single sentence from the official historical record is worth dwelling on. It means that what began as intervention became presence, and what began as emergency became habit.

By 1912 the language was already familiar. President Taft congratulated the Navy and Marine Corps for "reestablishing order in Nicaragua,"[110] and the Congressional Research Service (CRS) later summarized the deployment for the same year in equally characteristic terms: U.S. forces protected American interests during an attempted revolution, while a smaller force remained afterward as a legation guard and in the service of

---

[108] Office of the Historian, U.S. Department of State, "Dollar Diplomacy, 1909–1913," identifying Nicaragua as a principal example of Taft-Knox policy; see also Nicaragua country page summarizing long Marine presence and recurrent diplomatic involvement.

[109] Office of the Historian, U.S. Department of State, "Nicaragua," noting that Zelaya resigned on December 17, 1909 and that the Marines remained stationed in Nicaragua until 1932, aside from a nine-month period in 1925–1926.

[110] William Howard Taft, annual message for 1912, congratulating American naval and Marine forces for "reestablishing order in Nicaragua".

"peace and stability."[111] This is precisely the sort of language that concerns a book like this. It does not say war. It says order, interests, stability. Yet the reality beneath the words was armed intervention and a long military presence.

The second major phase came in 1926 and after. The CRS inventory records Marine landings in May 1926 and then a larger deployment from August 27, 1926 to January 3, 1933, after the Chamorro coup set off renewed revolutionary conflict.[112] During this period the United States did something more ambitious than mere temporary policing. It helped build a local instrument of force. The State Department's *Foreign Relations* volumes for 1927 identify a formal agreement establishing the Guardia Nacional de Nicaragua and a linked American role in suppressing what official documents then described as "bandit activities."[113] Here the shadow constitution deepened. Force was no longer simply American force. It was American force reorganizing Nicaraguan force.

That distinction matters because it marks a change in method. Occupation, by itself, is visible and finite. The creation of a constabulary or national guard is more enduring. It shifts the means of coercion into local hands while leaving the imprint of outside design. In Nicaragua, the man who came to symbolize armed resistance to this order was Augusto César Sandino. His

---

[111] CRS, *Instances of Use of United States Armed Forces Abroad*, describing the 1912 intervention as protection of American interests during an attempted revolution, followed by a continuing legation guard in support of peace and stability.

[112] Congressional Research Service, *Instances of Use of United States Armed Forces Abroad*, listing Marine landings in May 1926 and from August 27, 1926 to January 3, 1933, after the Chamorro coup and ensuing revolutionary activity.

[113] Office of the Historian, *Foreign Relations of the United States, 1927*, index entries for the agreement establishing the Guardia Nacional and for U.S. Marine assistance in suppressing "bandit activities"; see also the July 16, 1927 Ocotal attack document.

attack on the Marine and constabulary garrison at Ocotal in July 1927 made him the emblem of anti-interventionist nationalism, even as Washington and its local allies treated his movement as a form of disorder to be put down.

When the Marines finally withdrew in January 1933, the constitutional story did not end. It merely changed hands. The United States transferred control to a Nicaraguan national force it had helped shape. Within a year Sandino had been killed. State Department documents from 1934 record both the suspicion that Somoza was responsible and the later acknowledgment that Sandino and his associates had indeed been killed.[114] What followed was not a stable republic liberated from intervention, but the rise of the Somoza order. By 1936, State Department memoranda were already discussing whether the United States should recognize a Somoza regime if it effectively governed and fulfilled international obligations, regardless of older treaty scruples.[115] The cycle had become unmistakable: intervention, tutelage, withdrawal, client force, and durable local authoritarianism.

This middle phase of the Nicaraguan story is essential to the later one, because the 20th-century Sandinistas took their name from Sandino himself. The revolution that overthrew the Somoza dictatorship in 1979 therefore returned Nicaragua to American strategic concern under conditions laden with memory. The Carter administration faced a collapsing Somoza regime, revolutionary forces moving toward victory, and the question whether Nicaragua would become another node in a

---

[114] Office of the Historian, *Foreign Relations of the United States, 1934*, documents recording strong suspicion that Somoza had Sandino killed and later acknowledgment that Sandino and his associates had been killed.

[115] Office of the Historian, *Foreign Relations of the United States, 1936*, memorandum stating that under the newer policy the United States would recognize a Somoza regime if it effectively governed the country and fulfilled its international obligations.

widening Cold War struggle. The State Department's historical summary of Central America for the Carter years notes that the Sandinista movement prevailed in July 1979 and that Nicaragua's example shaped regional fears of revolutionary spread.[116] On the very day of the Sandinista triumph, Carter signed a covert finding directing the CIA to assist "democratic elements" in Nicaragua against Marxist consolidation and Cuban influence.[117] Even before Reagan, the old habit had returned: Nicaragua was again being managed not primarily through formal war, but through covert and semi-covert means.

The Reagan years brought the pattern into even clearer relief. A *Foreign Relations* document from 1981–1982 states the administration's view with unusual candor: diplomatic pressure alone would not suffice, and policy had to "take the war to Nicaragua."[118] That phrase deserves to be read slowly. It is the modern equivalent of the older vocabulary of order and stability, but with a different emphasis. Nicaragua was once again a place where the United States sought to fight indirectly, through proxies, pressure, and managed escalation rather than through declaration of war.

The State Department's own historical summary of Central America from 1981 to 1993 records the result in public terms. Congress eventually approved $100 million in aid for the Contras

---

[116] Office of the Historian, U.S. Department of State, "Central America, 1977–1980," noting the Sandinista victory in July 1979 and the wider regional implications of the Nicaraguan revolution; the same summary describes the Somoza dictatorship's decay and the political explosion after the 1972 Managua earthquake.

[117] Office of the Historian, *Foreign Relations of the United States, 1977–1980*, vol. XV, document 305, stating that on July 19, 1979 President Carter signed a covert finding directing the CIA to assist democratic elements in Nicaragua against Marxist consolidation.

[118] Office of the Historian, *Foreign Relations of the United States, 1981–1988*, vol. I, document 166, stating that diplomatic pressure alone would not be enough and that policy had to "take the war to Nicaragua."

in 1986, but the Iran-Contra scandal broke the next month.[119] That scandal belongs properly to the next chapter. Here the larger point is enough: Nicaragua had become, once more, a theater in which the United States acted under conditions of constitutional ambiguity — this time not through Marines and legation guards, but through covert operations, proxy forces, and contested appropriations.

Seen in long perspective, Nicaragua reveals something larger than a series of interventions. It reveals a recurring American habit. The country repeatedly invited action not because it was uniquely important in itself at every moment, but because it lay at the intersection of strategic imagination, ideological fear, and executive flexibility. There the United States could intervene, stabilize, supervise, pressure, arm, or proxy-fight without the older public form of declared war. Nicaragua thus became a laboratory for what this book calls the shadow constitution: armed action in the penumbra between open war and open peace.

The older interventions were public and military. The later ones became indirect and covert. But the constitutional family resemblance is unmistakable. In each era, Nicaragua was treated as a place where force might be used in the name of order, security, or larger strategic necessity without requiring the republic to pass through the full formal threshold of war.

That is why Nicaragua repeats.

---

[119] Office of the Historian, U.S. Department of State, "Central America, 1981–1993," noting congressional approval of $100 million for the Contras in 1986 and the outbreak of the Iran-Contra scandal the following month.

# Chapter 13:
# Iran-Contra and
# the Appropriations Constitution

If Nicaragua is a repeating theater, Iran–Contra is the moment at which that theater turned constitutional.

The United States had intervened in Nicaragua before, with Marines, legation guards, constabularies, and proxy structures. But the constitutional issue posed by the Iran–Contra affair was not simply whether the Executive might again act forcefully in Central America. It was whether the Executive might sustain a foreign policy that Congress had refused to fund.

Congress itself had already crossed a threshold before the confrontation began. In the early 1980s it authorized and funded assistance to the Nicaraguan Contra movement as part of the broader Cold War struggle in Central America. Some observers noted the novelty of this step: the United States was now openly supporting an armed insurgent force seeking to overthrow a government with which it still maintained diplomatic relations and technically remained at peace.[120] Congress soon reconsidered the policy, however, and beginning in 1982 enacted a series of restrictions — collectively known as the Boland Amendments — limiting or prohibiting U.S. assistance to the Contras.

---

[120] E. Bradford Burns, *At War in Nicaragua: The United States and the Nicaraguan Revolution* (New York: Harper & Row, 1987), ch. 1. Burns observed that congressional funding of the Contra insurgency represented a new step in U.S. policy: supporting an armed movement seeking to overthrow a government with which the United States maintained diplomatic relations.

Congress had used this power before. Only a decade earlier it had relied on the same constitutional authority — the power of the purse — to terminate American combat operations in Vietnam. The Constitution's language on that point is blunt: "No Money shall be drawn from the Treasury, but in Consequence of Appropriations made by Law."[121] That clause does more than regulate bookkeeping. It gives Congress the hardest and most practical control a legislature can possess over policy, including foreign and military policy. Presidents may speak, command, persuade, and propose. But if Congress refuses to appropriate money, the policy is supposed to stop.

That is why the Boland restrictions mattered so much. They were not a single enactment but a series of provisions, changing over time, through which Congress attempted to limit support for the Nicaraguan Contras. From late 1982 into late 1983 there was a prohibition on CIA and Defense Department expenditures aimed at overthrowing the Nicaraguan government or provoking a Nicaragua–Honduras war. From late 1983 into October 1984 Congress capped assistance at $24 million. From October 3, 1984 to December 19, 1985, a stricter prohibition barred the expenditure of funds by the CIA, the Department of Defense, or any other U.S. entity involved in intelligence activities to support the Contras' military or paramilitary effort.[122]

The constitutional question sharpened in that strict phase. Once the President signed the 1984 continuing appropriations bill containing the Boland restriction, the Executive no longer faced a mere political disagreement with Congress. It faced enacted law.

---

[121] U.S. Const. art. I, §9, cl. 7.

[122] Ronald Reagan Presidential Library, summary memorandum of Boland Amendment provisions.

Yet the policy did not stop. The joint congressional committees investigating what later became known as the Iran–Contra affair summarized the turn with unusual force. After the 1984 restriction became law, President Reagan still felt strongly about the Contras and, in the words of his National Security Adviser, ordered his staff to find a way to keep the Contras' "body and soul together." The committees concluded that the affair revealed a deeper institutional failure: the United States had come to pursue a public foreign policy and a covert one simultaneously.[123]

The committees then drew the crucial institutional conclusion: "Thus began the story of how the staff of a White House advisory body, the NSC, became an operational entity that secretly ran the Contra assistance effort, and later the Iran initiative."[124]

What followed raised an additional constitutional issue beyond the Boland restrictions themselves. The covert program was sustained in part through proceeds from the secret sale of U.S. Government arms to Iran. Instead of returning those funds to the Treasury through the normal appropriations process, some of the proceeds were diverted to support the Contra effort.[125]

The congressional committees concluded that this diversion of government-controlled funds in order to sustain a policy that

---

[123] Report of the Congressional Committees Investigating the Iran–Contra Affair, S. Rep. No. 100-216 / H. Rep. No. 100-433 (1987), Executive Summary.

[124] *Iran–Contra Report*, Narrative Report.

[125] The covert arms transfers to Iran were initially undertaken in part in the hope that Iranian intermediaries would assist in securing the release of American hostages held in Lebanon during the mid-1980s. During these operations, proceeds from some of the arms sales were later diverted to support the Nicaraguan Contra forces, producing the Iran–Contra controversy.

Congress had restricted amounted to a violation of the Appropriations Clause of the Constitution.[126]

That conclusion goes to the heart of the episode. Iran–Contra was not only a matter of arms and hostages. It was also a matter of institutional mutation. A body created to advise and coordinate became a body that implemented, solicited, transferred, concealed, and managed. The statutory purpose of the National Security Council was to "advise the President with respect to the integration of domestic, foreign, and military policies relating to the national security."[127] The affair showed how far that advisory role had drifted.

The methods by which the Contra effort was sustained were equally revealing. Once denied funding by Congress, the Administration turned to third countries and private sources. By circumventing Congress's power of the purse through foreign contributions and other channels, the committees concluded, the administration had undermined "a cardinal principle of the Constitution."[128]

Defenders of the Administration advanced a narrower legal argument. A minority statement attached to the joint committee report maintained that the Boland Amendment was an appropriations rider and that there was no clear evidence that substantial appropriated funds had been used to sustain the Contra effort. Some officials also argued that the National Security Council staff believed, not implausibly, that the strict Boland prohibition did not cover the NSC itself. In this view, most NSC staff activities were lawful except perhaps the diversion of Iran arms-sale proceeds to the resistance.[129]

---

[126] *Iran–Contra Report,* Findings and Conclusions.
[127] National Security Act of 1947, 50 U.S.C. §3021.
[128] *Iran–Contra Report,* Findings and Conclusions.
[129] *Iran–Contra Report,* Minority Views.

That argument should not be ignored. It captures the strongest technical defense offered at the time. But the larger constitutional question is not so easily reduced to statutory interpretation. The issue was whether the Executive could preserve a prohibited policy by shifting its financing outside of the ordinary appropriations process — through foreign governments, private intermediaries, and proceeds from the sale of government arms. Once that move is allowed, Congress's "power of the purse" begins to lose its practical meaning.

This is why the title of the chapter is not simply *Iran–Contra and the Boland Amendment.* The deeper issue is what might be called the appropriations constitution itself. If Congress's final lever can be evaded whenever the Executive is determined enough and resourceful enough, then one of the founders' principal safeguards against unilateral policy is weakened at the root.

The public revelation of the diversion came in November 1986. Attorney General Edwin Meese announced that proceeds from the secret sale of U.S. arms to Iran had been diverted to support the Contras.[130] Once exposed, the arrangement immediately raised not only criminal and political questions but a constitutional one: whether covert foreign policy could be insulated from Congress by being financed outside the visible channels of law.

Both the Tower Commission and the joint congressional committees treated the institutional lesson as severe. The committees recommended that members and staff of the National Security Council should not engage in covert operations and further recommended legislation clarifying that a

---

[130] Statement of Attorney General Edwin Meese, Nov. 25, 1986.

presidential finding cannot authorize any action inconsistent with a statute of the United States.[131]

There is a final irony worth noting. In October 1986, just before the scandal became public, Congress again approved $100 million in military assistance for the Contras. That fact does not erase the constitutional issue. It sharpens it. The point of Iran–Contra was not that Congress would never support the policy. The point was that during the period when Congress had withdrawn its support — and had prohibited funding — elements of the Executive sought to preserve the policy anyway.

The Iran–Contra is more than a scandal of secrecy. It is a case study in the temptation to treat appropriations control as an obstacle to be engineered around. It shows how quickly an advisory body can become operational when policy is to be maintained despite law; how easily foreign money and private intermediaries can be used to cloud responsibility; and how fragile legislative control becomes if its strongest check can be bypassed rather than confronted.

In constitutional form, the lesson is stark. Congress' control of money is not a technical detail. It is one of the main ways a republic prevents foreign policy from slipping wholly into executive discretion. Iran–Contra did not abolish that principle. It demonstrated how much damage can be done when officials try to preserve a policy after Congress has used the one weapon the Constitution most clearly gave it to stop the policy: the refusal to pay for it.

---

[131] *Iran–Contra Report,* Findings and Conclusions.

# Chapter 14:
# Intelligence, Covert Action, and the Operational State

The constitutional story has now tested, one by one, the principal levers by which a republic was meant to govern the use of force. Declaration has faded. Authorization has stretched. Consultation and withdrawal procedures have proved uncertain. Appropriations have remained the hardest check, but even that check has been tested by efforts at circumvention. The constitutional structure still stands, but it no longer operates in the clean, public sequence the founders most readily would have recognized.

For alongside the visible constitutional machinery of Congress and the Presidency, another structure has grown — less public, more specialized, often secret, and sometimes operational in a sense the older constitutional vocabulary did not fully anticipate. The growth of intelligence agencies, covert action authorities, and national-security staffs did not abolish the Constitution. But it changed the practical environment in which the Constitution's war powers now operate. The question is no longer only who may declare, authorize, fund, or command open war. It is also who may plan, direct, conceal, and sustain action below the threshold of formal war and outside the ordinary channels of public accountability.

*The Constitutional Levers*

It is worth pausing, briefly, to notice the position at which the book has now arrived.

Korea showed that the republic could fight a major war without a declaration. Vietnam showed that a broad congressional authorization could become a warrant for prolonged escalation. The War Powers Resolution represented Congress' attempt to recover ground through consultation, reporting, and withdrawal deadlines. Iran–Contra then exposed the most severe confrontation of all: an effort by elements of the Executive to sustain a prohibited policy after Congress had used the Constitution's hardest instrument, the power of the purse, to stop it.

Taken together, these episodes reveal something larger than any single controversy. The constitutional levers remain in place, but each has been stretched, adapted, or challenged in practice. This does not mean the constitutional system has collapsed. It means that the center of gravity has moved. The next stage of the story lies in that movement.

### The Rise of the Operational State

The birth of the modern operational state is usually dated, for good reason, to 1947.

The National Security Act of that year created the National Security Council and the Central Intelligence Agency. The statutory role of the NSC was advisory: it was to "advise the President with respect to the integration of domestic, foreign, and military policies relating to the national security."[132] The original intelligence structure was also described in terms that appeared limited. The CIA was not to exercise "police, subpoena, law-enforcement powers, or internal-security

---

[132] National Security Act of 1947, as amended, 50 U.S.C. § 3021. The statute provides that the National Security Council shall "advise the President with respect to the integration of domestic, foreign, and military policies relating to the national security."

functions." At the same time, however, the statute and its immediate antecedents contained a clause of lasting consequence: the intelligence apparatus could perform "such other functions and duties related to intelligence affecting the national security" as the National Security Council might direct.[133]

That phrase, modest in appearance, opened the constitutional door through which covert action soon entered.

Within a year, the National Security Council moved through it. In June 1948, NSC 10/2 authorized a covert operations program and created within the CIA the Office of Policy Coordination. According to later CIA histories and declassified materials, the new directive authorized activities including propaganda, political action, economic warfare, sabotage, subversion, assistance to underground resistance movements and guerrillas, and support to anti-communist elements abroad. It also contemplated that such operations would be conducted so that, if uncovered, the United States could plausibly disclaim responsibility.[134]

That last point is crucial. The covert-action system was not just secret in the ordinary sense of classified military planning. It was designed for deniability. Its political logic differed from

---

[133] The original National Security Act and its immediate antecedents combined two principles that would remain in tension: the CIA would have no "police, subpoena, law-enforcement powers, or internal-security functions," but could perform "such other functions and duties related to intelligence affecting the national security" as the NSC might direct. See *The National Security Act of 1947* (CIA Reading Room); see also current codification at 50 U.S.C. § 3036(d)(1), (4).

[134] NSC 10/2, issued June 18, 1948, created the Office of Policy Coordination and broadly defined covert operations to include propaganda, economic warfare, sabotage, subversion, assistance to underground resistance movements and guerrillas, and related activities; CIA historical materials also note that such operations were to be conducted so that U.S. responsibility could be plausibly disclaimed if uncovered.

overt force from the beginning. When Congress declares war, the republic openly changes its condition. When covert action is used, the state seeks to act without openly acknowledging that it has acted.

This was the beginning of the operational state in its modern form: not only intelligence gathering, but an organized capacity to shape events abroad through secret means while preserving a public posture of distance or ambiguity.

The distinction between intelligence and operations soon became difficult to maintain. Intelligence, in its strictest sense, gathers, evaluates, and transmits information. Covert action seeks political effect. Once both are housed in the same institutional family, the boundary between knowing and doing, collecting and acting, becomes harder to police. This is not simply a bureaucratic issue. It is constitutional in consequence. A republic may be able to accommodate secret collection more easily than secret operations, because the latter begin to approximate a form of war or intervention without the older political rites that overt force would require.

The Cold War encouraged precisely that development. Covert action seemed to offer a middle path between diplomacy and war, between passivity and open intervention. It promised influence without occupation, effect without declaration, pressure without full mobilization. That made it attractive not only strategically but constitutionally, because it appeared to avoid the public thresholds that declarations or overt campaigns required. Yet that very attraction is what made it dangerous to republican accountability.

The Church Committee's investigations in the mid-1970s exposed the darker side of this system. In its interim report on assassination plots, the Senate committee found that "the evidence establishes that the United States was implicated in several assassination plots" involving foreign leaders.[135] In its Chile staff report, the committee described covert action in Chile between 1963 and 1973 as "extensive and continuous," involving millions of dollars in efforts to influence elections, shape institutions, and affect the political outcome of a sovereign state.[136] These findings did not reveal a few stray abuses at the edges of an otherwise tidy system. They revealed a standing capability for secret political intervention.

The Chile report is especially useful for this chapter because it shows how broad the category of covert action had become. The committee said the CIA's activities in Chile ranged across propaganda, support for political parties and media, influence operations directed at labor, students, and other institutions, and covert ties to domestic factions and military actors.[137] The intelligence apparatus had become a practical instrument of political action abroad. At that point, to speak of "intelligence" alone was already misleading.

Congress responded with oversight reforms. The Hughes–Ryan Amendment of 1974 required that the President report covert CIA operations in a foreign country to the relevant congressional committees and, in practice, compelled the use of

---

[135] Senate Select Committee to Study Governmental Operations with Respect to Intelligence Activities (Church Committee), *Interim Report: Alleged Assassination Plots Involving Foreign Leaders*, S. Rep. No. 94-465 (1975), stating that the evidence established U.S. implication in several assassination plots.

[136] Church Committee, staff report, *Covert Action in Chile, 1963–1973* (1975). The report states that the facts presented were intended to lay out the basic facts of covert action in Chile and described U.S. covert involvement there as "extensive and continuous," including spending to influence elections, parties, media, and institutions.

[137] Church Committee, staff report, *Covert Action in Chile, 1963–1973* (1975), detailing CIA activities including propaganda, political funding, influence operations directed at labor and student groups, and covert relationships with domestic political and military actors.

formal presidential findings.[138] The Intelligence Oversight Act of 1980 then narrowed and regularized the reporting structure, concentrating notice to the intelligence committees rather than the wider spread of committees that had been involved under Hughes–Ryan.[139] The investigations also produced an executive prohibition on political assassination, first issued in 1976 and reaffirmed by subsequent administrations.[140] The current covert-action statute, now codified at 50 U.S.C. §3093, reflects this post-Church effort at legalization. It provides that the President may not authorize covert action unless he determines in a written finding that it is necessary to support identifiable foreign policy objectives and important to national security; it further states that a finding may not authorize or sanction a covert action, or any aspect of one, that has already occurred.[141]

Those provisions are important, but they should not be misunderstood. They do not abolish covert action. They regulate it. They attempt to force secrecy into procedural channels— finding, notice, committees, legal consultation — without

---

[138] Senate Select Committee on Intelligence, *The Role of Intelligence* (committee history), noting that the Hughes–Ryan Amendment "for the first time required that the President report any covert CIA operations in a foreign country" to the relevant congressional committees.

[139] CIA historical account of congressional oversight notes that the Intelligence Oversight Act of 1980 superseded the broader Hughes–Ryan reporting practice by limiting reporting of covert actions to the two intelligence committees; see also related committee histories.

[140] The Church Committee revelations concerning assassination plots led to the first formal prohibition on assassination in Executive Order 11905 (1976), later reaffirmed in Executive Orders 12036 (1978) and 12333 (1981), which provide that no person employed by or acting on behalf of the United States Government shall engage in or conspire to engage in assassination.

[141] 50 U.S.C. § 3093. The statute provides that the President may not authorize a covert action unless he signs a finding determining that it is necessary to support identifiable foreign policy objectives and important to national security; it also states that, except in narrow circumstances requiring immediate action, a finding may not authorize or sanction a covert action, or any aspect of one, that has already occurred.

eliminating the operational capability itself. The result is not the end of the operational state, but its statutory domestication.

Iran–Contra showed how incomplete that domestication was. As the previous chapter demonstrated, the problem was not only covert action but institutional drift: the NSC staff, whose statutory role was advisory, became operational in practice. That is a revealing development because it means the operational state acquired more than one head. There was not only the CIA's covert-action machinery. There was also the national-security staff around the President, increasingly capable of planning, coordinating, and sustaining operations through channels that were neither fully military nor fully legislative.

This multiplication of channels matters constitutionally. The older constitutional text imagines, broadly speaking, Congress and the Executive. The modern security system distributes real operational capacity among the President, the NSC staff, the intelligence agencies, and, in other contexts, military special operations and allied or proxy forces. The more such capacity is distributed through secret or semi-secret channels, the harder it becomes for the old public levers — declaration, open authorization, visible appropriations, and civic assent — to operate with their earlier force.

That does not mean covert action is always illegitimate or always unwise. A serious nation will sometimes need secrecy. Intelligence collection is indispensable, and some operations may indeed be impracticable if wholly public. The constitutional problem is different. It is that secret operations are harder to align with republican accountability than overt ones. They are easier to deny, easier to compartmentalize, easier to finance obscurely, and easier to conduct without forcing the republic to acknowledge what it is doing.

For that reason, the institutional location of operations matters. Military action, however controversial, ordinarily moves through clearer chains of command, more visible appropriations, and a more developed body of law. Over time the armed services have also developed internal legal structures—rules of engagement, judge-advocate review, and established operational doctrine—that embed legal constraint directly into the conduct of operations.

The covert-action system developed differently. Its restraints were less institutional and more procedural: presidential findings, classified reporting to congressional committees, and internal executive review. These mechanisms attempted to introduce oversight without abandoning secrecy, but they did not replicate the older, embedded legal framework that had evolved within the military establishment. In this sense, procedural oversight came to substitute for the institutional safeguards that had traditionally governed military operations. When operational authority shifts into institutions governed primarily by secrecy and procedure rather than visible chains of command, the relationship between secrecy and accountability becomes more precarious.

This is the larger meaning of the operational state. It is not a conspiracy theory, nor a mere slogan. It is the historical result of adding to the visible constitutional structure a parallel machinery of secret collection, covert action, advisory staffs with operational reach, and statutory procedures meant to legalize secrecy without fully publicizing it. A republic can live with such a system. The harder question is whether it can govern it in the older constitutional spirit.

The answer, so far, is mixed. Congress has investigated, legislated, and demanded notice. Courts have occasionally checked executive overreach. Presidents still seek legal justifications and written findings. Yet the basic fact remains: once the state acquires a standing capacity to act covertly, the constitutional problem of war and peace no longer lies only in open decisions for war. It also lies in the quiet accumulation of operational power in institutions that were not originally supposed to command the field.

The modern Executive is therefore no longer a single constitutional hand. It has become, in effect, a many-headed operational apparatus. The founders feared the concentration of war power in one magistrate. The modern republic faces a different but related danger: the diffusion of operational power through institutions whose secrecy and specialization make ordinary republican checks harder to apply.

The next step in the story lies just beyond the state itself. We now turn to the rise of private force, contractors, and the growing blur between war and policing.

# Chapter 15:
## Private Force, Privateering, and the Police-War Border

The modern operational state does not end at the edge of the state itself. It reaches outward.

That is the next constitutional development to trace. Once force can be organized through covert channels, intelligence services, advisory staffs, and proxy arrangements, it is only a short step further to force carried by actors who are neither ordinary soldiers nor ordinary civil officers. At that point, the republic confronts not simply the problem of secrecy, but the problem of **delegated violence**. Who may lawfully carry force on behalf of the state? Through what chain of command? Under what law? And when such force is used, is the republic at war, engaged in law enforcement, or something uneasily in between?

The Constitution itself anticipated at least one form of delegated violence. Article I gives Congress the power to "grant Letters of Marque and Reprisal."[142] That clause now sounds archaic, but it deserves more respect than modern ears might give it. A letter of marque was a public commission authorizing a private party to engage in what would otherwise be piracy: the capture of enemy shipping and goods under the law of prize.[143] The point is not simply that the founders inherited the practice.

---

[142] U.S. Const. art. I, § 8, cl. 11, giving Congress the power to "declare War, grant Letters of Marque and Reprisal, and make Rules concerning Captures on Land and Water."

[143] A letter of marque was a government license authorizing privateering; captured vessels were subject to prize law. See Legal Information Institute, "letter of marque."

The point is that even private force, when used in national service, was treated as a matter of public authorization. Delegated violence remained subject to an open legislative act.

That is a revealing constitutional choice. The founders did not imagine that private actors could wage war for the republic simply because the executive found them useful. Even the privateer required public commission. The state might delegate force, but it did so openly and through law.

During the 19th century, most maritime powers moved away from privateering. The Declaration of Paris of 1856[144] renounced the practice among the states that acceded to it, and the declaration itself provided that it would bind only those powers that accepted it. The United States never formally became a party. The constitutional clause therefore remained in place, even as privateering fell out of practical use. That fact matters because it leaves behind a kind of historical fossil. The Constitution still remembers a form of private war, but it remembers it as something that required Congressional grant, not executive improvisation.

The modern equivalent is not privateering in the old sense. Private military contractors do not capture prizes under letters of marque, and they do not operate through admiralty courts. But the family resemblance is still worth noticing. They are private actors, often armed, often hired for profit, performing functions once carried more plainly within military structures. If the old privateer was a legally commissioned private instrument of war, the modern contractor is a privately hired instrument of security, logistics, protection, and, at times, force.

Nowhere did that development become more visible than in Iraq. The Congressional Budget Office reported that by early 2008 approximately 25,000 to 30,000 employees of private

---

[144] The Declaration Respecting Maritime Law (Paris, 1856).

security contractors were operating in Iraq, with about 10,000 of them working directly for the U.S. government.[145] That scale was extraordinary. These were not scattered civilian adjuncts at the margin of a campaign. They formed a standing armed presence around military and diplomatic operations.

Their legal position was equally revealing. Coalition Provisional Authority Order 17, issued in 2004, provided that contractors would be immune from Iraqi legal process for acts performed pursuant to the terms and conditions of their contracts.[146] The order did not abolish all law. Congress had already enacted the Military Extraterritorial Jurisdiction Act of 2000 to provide federal criminal jurisdiction over certain offenses committed outside the United States by persons employed by or accompanying the armed forces.[147] But the resulting framework was markedly different from the older military one. Contractors were not governed by the full, settled structure of military law. Their accountability depended instead on a patchwork of contract status, immunities, executive arrangements, and later criminal jurisdiction.

The Nisour Square shootings of September 16, 2007 made that problem impossible to ignore. Four former Blackwater security guards were later convicted in federal court of charges stemming from the shooting in Baghdad, which the Justice Department said resulted in the killing of 14 unarmed civilians and the wounding of numerous others.[148] The convictions

---

[145] Congressional Budget Office, Contractors' Support of U.S. Operations in Iraq (2008).

[146] Coalition Provisional Authority Order No. 17 (Revised), § 4(3).

[147] Military Extraterritorial Jurisdiction Act of 2000, Pub. L. 106-523, establishing federal jurisdiction over certain criminal offenses committed outside the United States by persons employed by or accompanying the armed forces.

[148] U.S. Department of Justice, "Four Former Blackwater Employees Found Guilty of Charges in Fatal Nisur Square Shooting in Iraq" (2014), and "Former Blackwater Employee Sentenced to Life Imprisonment…"

mattered because they showed that private force was not beyond all legal reach. Yet the episode also showed how indirect and belated that reach could be. This was accountability after the fact, through extraordinary and controversial prosecution, not the ordinary embedded discipline of a standing military chain of command.

The problem with private force is not simply that private actors carry weapons. It is that when operational roles migrate outward from the military into the world of contracts and executive hiring, the legal structure changes with them. Institutional military oversight gives way to contract management, extraterritorial statutes, immunity provisions, and after-the-fact prosecutions. The state has not renounced responsibility, but it has made responsibility harder to locate.

This modern use of private force differs in another important respect from the constitutional model of letters of marque. The old privateer was at least openly licensed by Congress. The modern contractor is typically hired through executive agencies, often for functions described as security, escort, or support rather than war. The delegation remains real, but the public constitutional act is missing. In that sense, the modern republic has not revived privateering. It has improvised a more administrative, less explicit form of private force.

The same blurring appears when war begins to resemble policing.

The case of Manuel Noriega is the clearest example. In February 1988, a federal grand jury in Florida indicted the Panamanian leader on drug-trafficking charges.[149] Less than two

---

(2019). DOJ stated that the shooting resulted in the deaths of 14 unarmed civilians and numerous injuries.

[149] *United States v. Noriega*, 683 F. Supp. 1373 (S.D. Fla. 1988), stating that Noriega was indicted in the Southern District of Florida in February 1988

years later, on December 20, 1989, President George H. W. Bush ordered U.S. military action in Panama. In his address to the nation, Bush justified the operation on four grounds: safeguarding American lives, defending democracy in Panama, combating drug trafficking, and protecting the integrity of the Panama Canal treaties.[150] The operation, known as Just Cause, did not end with the mere defeat of hostile armed units. Noriega ultimately surrendered, was brought to Miami, and entered the criminal process of the United States.[151]

This is not ordinary war in the old constitutional sense, nor is it ordinary law enforcement. It is something between them: military force used in part to achieve what law enforcement alone could not accomplish, including the capture of an indicted foreign ruler. That is the police-war border.

The constitutional significance of that border is easy to miss because the practical case against Noriega was strong and the military action was quickly successful. Yet the form of the episode deserves attention. A foreign leader against whom the United States remained formally at peace was first indicted in federal court and then removed by invasion. The categories of war and policing had begun to overlap. Force once associated with public war was now serving ends associated with arrest, prosecution, and criminal punishment.

This overlap has several consequences. First, it encourages the executive branch to speak of military action in police-like language: capture, extradition, criminality, trafficking, enforcement. Second, it makes the use of force seem less like war

---

on drug-trafficking charges. See also the ICRC case study on *United States v. Noriega.*

[150] George H. W. Bush, "Address to the Nation Announcing United States Military Action in Panama," Dec. 20, 1989.

[151] Government Printing Office news release, "Noriega in Miami for arraignment" (Jan. 4, 1990), and later litigation in *Noriega v. Pastrana* and related cases.

and more like an extension of public order. Third, it complicates the constitutional vocabulary of Congress's war powers, because the action may be defended less as war than as enforcement, rescue, or security.

That is why private force and the police-war border belong together. Both represent ways in which the republic's use of force moves outside the older public grammar of declared war. In one case, armed capacity shifts outward into contractors and private firms. In the other, military action shifts conceptually toward law enforcement and policing. The result in both cases is the same: the citizen sees less clearly when the nation has crossed from peace into war.

The founders' constitutional treatment of privateering is instructive precisely because it made delegated force visible. Congress had to authorize it. The modern system, by contrast, often diffuses force through contracts, executive arrangements, and hybrid justifications that obscure where responsibility lies. That does not mean every contractor is a privateer or every military intervention an arrest operation. It means the categories have blurred, and with them the constitutional clarity that once marked the republic's entry into organized violence.

This marks another step in the evolution traced so far. The old declaration has vanished. Authorization has stretched. Appropriations have been tested. The operational state has multiplied the number of channels through which force may be organized. Now force begins to move beyond the ordinary military framework itself — into contractors, proxies, and police-like missions.

A republic can survive such adaptations. The harder question is whether it can still see itself clearly while using them.

# Part V:
# Perpetual Emergency

# Chapter 16:
# The AUMF Republic

If Korea marked the eclipse of declaration and Vietnam showed how authorization could become a broad warrant for escalation, the era after September 11 completed a further transformation. The United States did not cease to involve Congress in decisions about war. What changed was the form of that involvement. Instead of declarations or narrow crisis resolutions, Congress increasingly relied on Authorizations for Use of Military Force — statutes broad enough to permit force, elastic enough to travel, and durable enough to outlive the conflicts that first produced them.

The result was a new constitutional pattern. Congress continued to vote, authorize, fund, and review military action. But it did so through instruments that allowed war to proceed without the older public act by which the republic openly declared that its condition had changed. The declaration had once marked the threshold between peace and war. The AUMF authorized force while leaving the nation, at least rhetorically, somewhere short of that formal boundary.

The first major step toward that condition came in the Persian Gulf crisis of 1991. Congress did not declare war against Iraq. Instead it enacted the Authorization for Use of Military Force Against Iraq Resolution, authorizing the President, subject to a presidential determination, to use the armed forces pursuant to U.N. Security Council Resolution 678 in order to implement the relevant Security Council resolutions and restore peace in the region.[152] When President George H. W. Bush signed it on January 14, 1991, he described it as congressional approval of the use of force consistent with the U.N. resolution and as the clearest possible message to Saddam Hussein that he must withdraw from Kuwait. In other words, Congress still acted before war, but it now acted through a conditional authorization framed within an international collective-security structure rather than through an old-fashioned declaration.

That difference should not be exaggerated. The 1991 authorization still resembled the older form in important respects. It was public, debated, connected to a specific crisis, and passed just before major combat. Yet it also pointed toward a new model. Congress no longer declared that the republic was at war. It authorized the President to use force if he judged the conditions met. That form was not entirely new. Earlier Congresses had at times authorized force without formal declaration, beginning with Congress's authorization of Jefferson's actions against Tripoli. What changed was its scale and persistence. Authorization became broader, more open-ended, and more capable of sustaining military action across time without renewed public decision. The constitutional threshold remained, but it had changed shape.

The change became much larger after September 11, 2001. Public Law 107-40 authorized the President to use "all necessary and appropriate force" against those "nations, organizations, or persons" he determined had planned, authorized, committed, or aided the attacks of September 11, or harbored those responsible, in order to prevent future acts of international

---

[152] *Authorization for Use of Military Force Against Iraq Resolution*, Pub. L. 102-1, § 2, Jan. 14, 1991, authorizing the President, subject to a determination, to use U.S. armed forces pursuant to U.N. Security Council Resolution 678;

terrorism against the United States.[153] The wording is one of the most consequential pieces of war legislation in American history. It did not name a state alone. It did not confine itself to a single battlefield. It did not terminate with the defeat of a named enemy government. It tied force to a set of actors and an ongoing purpose: the prevention of future terrorism.

This was a profound alteration in legal form. Congress had always been able to legislate broadly. But the older declaration model still carried with it a public sense that war had begun against an identifiable enemy. The 2001 AUMF created something different: a standing legal basis for force against organizations, persons, and, in later executive practice, "associated forces" across multiple theaters and over many years.

Successive administrations made exactly that argument. The Obama administration's 2016 report on the legal and policy frameworks guiding the use of military force stated that the 2001 AUMF "continues to provide the domestic legal authority" for force against al-Qaeda, the Taliban, and associated forces, and described military operations in Afghanistan, Iraq, Syria, Libya, Yemen, and Somalia under that broader post-9/11 framework.[154] The Biden administration's 2024 report to Congress continued in the same vein, stating that in 2023 U.S. forces had used

---

[153] *Authorization for Use of Military Force*, Pub. L. 107-40, Sept. 18, 2001, authorizing the President to use "all necessary and appropriate force" against those nations, organizations, or persons he determined were responsible for the attacks of September 11 or harbored those responsible.

[154] "Report on the Legal and Policy Frameworks Guiding the United States' Use of Military Force and Related National Security Operations" (Obama Administration, Dec. 5, 2016). The report states that the 2001 AUMF continues to provide domestic legal authority against al-Qaeda, the Taliban, and associated forces, and describes operations in Afghanistan, Iraq, Syria, Libya, Yemen, and Somalia. It also states that, as a matter of domestic law, the 2001 and 2002 AUMFs authorized operations against ISIL in Iraq and Syria.

military force in Iraq, Syria, and Somalia, that there had been "no change" in the list of forces lawfully targetable under the 2001 AUMF, and that the 2001 and 2002 AUMFs together supported force used in defense of U.S. and partner forces pursuing those missions.[155]

In short, the 2001 AUMF did not simply authorize the opening campaign in Afghanistan. It became a continuing domestic-law foundation for military action in multiple countries, against multiple groups, across multiple administrations, for more than two decades. That is the heart of the AUMF republic.

The 2002 Iraq AUMF extended the pattern. Public Law 107-243 authorized the President to use the armed forces "as he determines to be necessary and appropriate" to defend the national security of the United States against the continuing threat posed by Iraq and to enforce relevant U.N. Security Council resolutions. When signing it, President George W. Bush emphasized that Congress had "authorized the use of force," though he added that he had "not ordered the use of force" and hoped it would not become necessary.[156] Again, the crucial point is formal. Congress acted. But it acted not by declaration, and not by a narrow, self-expiring crisis statute. It enacted a broad

---

[155] "Report to Congress on the Legal and Policy Frameworks for the United States' Use of Military Force and Related National Security Operations" (Biden Administration, Mar. 1, 2024). The report states that in 2023 U.S. forces used military force in Iraq, Syria, and Somalia; that there had been "no change" in the list of forces targetable under the 2001 AUMF; and that the 2001 and 2002 AUMFs supported force used to carry out missions and defend U.S. and partner forces pursuing them.

[156] *Authorization for Use of Military Force Against Iraq Resolution of 2002*, Pub. L. 107-243, § 3, Oct. 16, 2002, authorizing the President to use the armed forces as he determined "necessary and appropriate" against the continuing threat posed by Iraq and to enforce relevant U.N. resolutions; George W. Bush, "President Signs Iraq Resolution," Oct. 16, 2002, stating that Congress had "authorized the use of force" though he had "not ordered the use of force."

authorization resting on executive determination and linked to both national-security judgment and international resolutions.

These authorizations altered not only how wars began but also what military force could legally support once underway. The 2001 AUMF, as interpreted by the executive branch and later acknowledged by Congress, underwrote detention authority as well as battlefield operations. President Bush's Military Order of November 13, 2001 invoked the AUMF in ordering the detention and trial by military commission of certain non-citizens in the war against terrorism.[157] President Obama later stated that section 1021 of the National Defense Authorization Act for Fiscal Year 2012 merely "affirms" authority already included in the 2001 AUMF to detain covered persons under the law of war.[158] In the AUMF republic, authorization does not simply open a campaign. It creates an enduring legal architecture around conflict — detention, targeting, and military operations across time and space.

The result is a republic that remains formally constitutional yet lives in a more continuous relation to force. Congress still votes. The President still commands. But the public threshold of war has become less visible. Instead of declaring war against Germany or Japan, the nation now lives under standing authorizations whose meaning is elaborated by executive branch lawyers, periodic War Powers reports, and later statutes that "affirm" rather than newly grant authority.

---

[157] George W. Bush, "Military Order of November 13, 2001: Detention, Treatment, and Trial of Certain Non-Citizens in the War Against Terrorism," invoking the AUMF as part of the legal basis for detention and military commission procedures.

[158] Barack Obama, "Statement on H.R. 1540," Dec. 31, 2011, stating that section 1021 of the National Defense Authorization Act for Fiscal Year 2012 "affirms" authority already included in the 2001 AUMF to detain covered persons under the law of war.

This is why the AUMF era cannot be understood simply as a change in drafting style. It changes the political experience of war. Declaration forced the republic to say plainly: war exists. AUMFs permit the republic to authorize force in advance, often broadly, and then allow the conflict to evolve through executive interpretation, appropriations, and reports to Congress. The legal basis remains. The civic rupture becomes less distinct.

The 2015 debate over the Islamic State made the point especially clear. President Obama wrote to Congress that although "existing statutes provide me with the authority I need" to use force against ISIL, he nevertheless sought a new AUMF as a matter of constitutional cooperation and political clarity.[159] Congress never enacted the requested authorization. Operations continued anyway, under the government's reading of the existing 2001 and 2002 AUMFs. Nothing better illustrates the mature AUMF republic. Congress's silence no longer necessarily meant the absence of authority. Old authorizations, interpreted expansively, could carry the policy forward.

This chapter is not arguing that all such uses of force were unlawful, nor that Congress was absent. It is making a narrower and more structural claim. The republic has moved from a system in which major war was expected to begin through declaration, to one in which force is increasingly initiated and sustained under broad authorizations that outlive the emergencies that produced them. That shift makes war less episodic, less public in legal form, and easier to normalize.

The earlier fear was concentration of war power in one magistrate. The AUMF republic presents a different but related

---

[159] Barack Obama, "Letter from the President — Authorization for the Use of United States Armed Forces in Connection with the Islamic State of Iraq and the Levant," Feb. 11, 2015, stating that "existing statutes provide me with the authority I need" while nonetheless requesting a new AUMF from Congress.

danger. Congress still acts, but it may act once and broadly; the President then interprets, extends, and operationalizes that authority over years and across theaters the original Congress never specifically contemplated. The public act remains congressional. The practical life of the authority becomes executive.

That is why the modern republic can appear both constitutional and perpetually at war.

# Chapter 17:
# Consent, Burden, and the All-Volunteer Republic

A republic's relation to war is governed not only by clauses, votes, and institutional forms. It is also governed by consent and burden.

Those two things are related, but they are not identical. A nation may authorize force through Congress while bearing its costs unequally. It may fight for years while most citizens remain untouched by compulsory service. It may sustain military operations abroad while ordinary civilian life continues with little visible alteration at home. That is one of the deepest transformations of the modern American system: the legal and political threshold of war has changed, but so has the social experience of war.

The older republic joined consent and burden more tightly. In the major conflicts of the first half of the 20th century, legislative action and mass mobilization still tended to move together. By the late 20th century and after, that connection had loosened. Three changes made the difference: the end of conscription, the disappearance of broad economic mobilization, and the rise of what may fairly be called an all-volunteer republic.

*The End of Conscription*

The older republic did more than authorize war. It distributed its burdens broadly enough that families, communities, and ordinary political life all felt the strain directly.

World War I brought 2,810,296 inductions through Selective Service. World War II brought 10,110,104. Korea brought 1,529,539. Vietnam brought 1,857,304.[160] These are not mere administrative statistics. They describe the civic structure of war. When war is fought through conscription, the republic does not merely consent to conflict; it makes the possibility of sacrifice widely and visibly present.

That did not mean earlier wars were fair in every respect. Vietnam in particular revealed the political toxicity of a draft that combined compulsion with deferments, exemptions, and visible inequalities. The Selective Service System later acknowledged that protest over "unfair deferments" became one of the central facts of the Vietnam era.[161] Yet even that injustice proves the point. The draft became politically explosive precisely because the burden was broad enough to matter and visible enough to be contested.

The transition away from that system came in the middle of the Vietnam period. In April 1970, Richard Nixon told Congress that the draft had begun as a temporary emergency measure before World War II and that too many Americans had come to accept it as a normal part of national life.[162] The Gates Commission, created to examine the issue, recommended an all-volunteer force, and Congress ultimately extended induction

---

160 Selective Service System, "Induction Statistics," listing 2,810,296 inductions in World War I, 10,110,104 in World War II, 1,529,539 in Korea, and 1,857,304 in Vietnam.

161 Selective Service System, "Historical Timeline," noting that during the Vietnam War the Selective Service encountered protest over "unfair deferments" and that it provided 20 percent of the men in uniform.

162 Richard Nixon, "Special Message to the Congress on Draft Reform," April 23, 1970, stating that the draft began as a temporary emergency measure before World War II and had come to be treated as a normal part of American life.

authority only until July 1, 1973.[163] The last man inducted entered the Army on June 30, 1973. From the next day forward, the United States depended on volunteers rather than conscripts.[164]

That change solved real problems. It ended a coercive system that had become increasingly divisive and, in many respects, arbitrary. It reduced one of the sharpest inequities of the Vietnam era and helped produce a highly professional military establishment. None of that should be denied. Yet constitutional history requires a second observation. The all-volunteer force also narrowed the military burden of war.

Once induction ended, the republic did not lose the machinery of national registration altogether. Registration resumed in July 1980 under Presidential Proclamation 4771, and it remains in effect as a standby system for men born in 1960 or later.[165] But a standby registration system is not the same thing as actual conscription. It preserves a latent obligation while withholding the active burden. The citizen is reminded that the nation may someday call, but for ordinary wars the call no longer comes.

That difference matters more than many legal debates acknowledge. The all-volunteer force changed not only how the United States staffed its military. It changed how the republic itself felt war.

---

[163] U.S. Department of Defense, *The Joint Chiefs of Staff and National Policy, 1969–1972*, describing the Gates Commission and its recommendation for an all-volunteer force; see also Selective Service System materials noting Congress's extension of induction authority until July 1, 1973.

[164] Selective Service System, "Induction Statistics," stating that the last man inducted entered the Army on June 30, 1973; see also Department of Defense historical materials noting that on July 1, 1973 the all-volunteer force formally began.

[165] Selective Service System, "Historical Timeline," stating that registration resumed in July 1980 under Presidential Proclamation 4771 and applies to men born in 1960 or later.

## The Disappearance of Mobilization

The narrowing of burden did not stop with military service. Earlier American wars, above all the Second World War, imposed broad economic obligations as well. Civilian life was reorganized by rationing of gasoline, rubber, sugar, and other goods; industry was redirected toward military production; and the federal government appealed directly to the public through war bond drives and other national campaigns.[166] War did not remain confined to the armed services. It reached into the household, the workplace, the consumer economy, and the ordinary routines of civilian life.

That wider burden did not eliminate profit. War has always created opportunities for industrial expansion and private gain. But in the older mobilization wars those gains were visibly offset by sacrifice. The nation knew itself to be at war not only because soldiers were fighting, but because civilian life had been reordered around the conflict. Rationing, bond purchases, production quotas, shortages, and shared inconvenience made war a public condition rather than a distant policy.

After 1945, that pattern largely faded. The United States maintained a large standing defense establishment, but military production increasingly became a permanent sector of the economy rather than a temporary wartime conversion. President Eisenhower captured the change in his 1961 farewell address when he warned that the nation now possessed "a permanent armaments industry of vast proportions."[167] He did not deny the

---

[166] See, e.g., David M. Kennedy, *Freedom from Fear: The American People in Depression and War, 1929–1945* (New York: Oxford University Press, 1999), on wartime rationing, industrial conversion, and war bond mobilization during World War II.

[167] Dwight D. Eisenhower, "Farewell Radio and Television Address to the American People," Jan. 17, 1961, warning of "a permanent armaments industry of vast proportions" and the political consequences of the military-industrial relationship.

necessity of such an establishment in the modern world. He warned that its economic and political weight had become a permanent feature of American life.

This was another reduction in civic friction. The republic could sustain military operations abroad without requiring comparable mobilization at home. No ration books appeared for Korea, Vietnam, Iraq, or Afghanistan. No national war bond culture reemerged. Consumer life remained largely intact. The economy of war became less a temporary civic conversion than a standing institutional arrangement.

That shift matters for the argument of this book because it changes the social meaning of consent. A republic may authorize war more readily when the economic structure of daily life no longer signals war as a visible departure from normality.

## The Volunteer Republic

The change in burden therefore extended beyond the armed forces themselves. The United States did not simply adopt an all-volunteer military. It moved toward what might be called an **all-volunteer civic posture toward war.**

Military service became voluntary. Broad economic sacrifice largely disappeared. Civic participation in war was increasingly reduced to taxation, symbolic support, media attention, and periodic political assent. The nation could therefore sustain military operations abroad while leaving ordinary life at home largely undisturbed. In this sense, the "all-volunteer force" described more than a manpower system. It described a wider transformation in the relationship between the republic and the wars fought in its name.

This helps explain the durability of the post-1973 system. Congress could still authorize force. Presidents could still command it. Public support could still surge in moments of direct attack, as it did after September 11, when the 2001 AUMF passed the Senate 98–0 and the House 420–1.[168] But consent no longer carried with it the same broad and immediate burdens that earlier wars had imposed. The wars that followed were fought by volunteers, repeated deployments, reserve components, and contractors rather than by mass induction and general mobilization. The nation was at war, but it was not mobilized in the older civic sense.

This is not an accusation against volunteers, nor a denial of the real strengths of a professional force. It is a constitutional observation about friction. The draft imposed friction. Economic mobilization imposed friction. Together they made war harder to abstract, harder to compartmentalize, and harder to leave to a professional minority. The all-volunteer republic reduced that friction. It did so for understandable reasons, and in some respects for good reasons. Yet the political consequence remains: war became easier to sustain as policy than as a shared civic condition.

That distinction helps explain one of the most curious features of modern American life: the coexistence of constant public honor for the military and a growing distance between military service and ordinary citizenship. The volunteer soldier becomes, at once, more respected and more socially separate. This has admirable elements, but it also has constitutional consequences. A republic risks allowing war to become the work of specialists — honored specialists, but specialists nonetheless — while the citizen body experiences conflict chiefly through language, symbolism, and appropriations rather than through direct obligation.

---

[168] U.S. Senate roll call vote on the 2001 AUMF, recording a 98–0 Senate vote; House passage by 420–1.

Seen in that light, the all-volunteer republic is not only a manpower arrangement. It is the social counterpart to the AUMF republic and the operational state. Declaration fades, authorization broadens, covert and private channels multiply, and at the same time the civic burden of war narrows. The result is a polity that can remain in military action for long periods without requiring the public to experience war as a rupture in ordinary life.

That is the final transformation this part of the book needed to show.

The republic now possesses standing authorizations, covert channels, operational staffs, private contractors, a professional volunteer military, and a permanent defense establishment. None of these developments alone abolishes constitutional government. Together, however, they make it easier for emergency to become normal. What was once war increasingly appears as policy, operation, campaign, or mission.

That is why perpetual emergency is not only a question of law. It is also a question of civic experience. A republic can live indefinitely in military action more easily when its citizens are asked for assent only intermittently and for sacrifice only unevenly.

The next and final question is therefore unavoidable: can a republic fight forever without ceasing, in some deeper sense, to live as a republic at peace?

# Conclusion

*Can a Republic Fight Forever?*

A republic can fight wars. It cannot abolish war power without abolishing sovereignty itself. The question has never been whether the United States should possess the means of defense. The question has always been how those means are distributed, restrained, acknowledged, and borne.

That was the founders' problem, and it remains ours.

The Constitution did not attempt to remove force from government. It divided the authority over force. Congress was given the powers to declare war, raise and support armies, provide and maintain a navy, regulate the armed forces, and control appropriations. The President was made Commander in Chief. The arrangement was neither accidental nor ornamental. It reflected a judgment about republican liberty: the decision to place the nation into war should not rest in a single hand, while the direction of forces once lawfully engaged required unity of command.[169]

The Convention's change from "make war" to "declare war" revealed the same design in miniature. Madison and Gerry's motion was meant to preserve the executive power to repel sudden attacks while withholding from the President a general authority to commence war. Ellsworth wanted it easier to get out of war than into it. Mason wanted to clog war rather than facilitate it. Hamilton later emphasized that the American President's power amounted to command, whereas the British

---

[169] U.S. Const. art. I, § 8, cls. 11–16; art. I, § 9, cl. 7; art. II, § 2, cl. 1.

king's power extended to declaring war and raising armies. Madison, writing afterward, was even blunter: the executive is the branch most interested in war and most prone to it.[170]

That was the constitutional settlement. The history that followed did not repeal it. It strained, bent, adapted, and in some respects obscured it.

The early republic largely still spoke the founders' language. Washington acted energetically to preserve peace without claiming a right to make war. Jefferson responded to attack in the Mediterranean, but refused to go beyond "the line of defence" without congressional sanction. Monroe, even after Jackson's successful Florida campaign, insisted that the Executive was incompetent to alter the nation's formal relation to Spain and that Congress alone possessed that power. These episodes did not eliminate ambiguity. They did, however, preserve the distinction between executive defense and legislative war.[171]

Jackson and Lincoln then revealed the two great temptations that would recur throughout the American story. Jackson showed how military success can create a fact on the ground faster than civilian government can comfortably absorb it. Lincoln showed the strongest possible case for emergency executive action: the preservation of the government itself in the midst of rebellion. Each exposed a real pressure within republican government. Jackson exposed the pressure of success; Lincoln the pressure of necessity. Neither, however, was a normal template for constitutional life. One was a frontier fait

---

[170] James Madison, *Notes of Debates in the Federal Convention of 1787*, Aug. 17, 1787; Alexander Hamilton, *The Federalist* No. 69; James Madison to Thomas Jefferson, Apr. 2, 1798.

[171] George Washington, Proclamation of Apr. 22, 1793; Thomas Jefferson, *First Annual Message to Congress*, Dec. 8, 1801; James Monroe, *Second Annual Message*, Nov. 16, 1818.

accompli later regularized by diplomacy. The other was civil war, in which the survival of the constitutional order itself was at stake.

The 20th century then brought the older constitutional model to its last great expression. In World War I and World War II, declarations of war still aligned with broad public assent and broad civic burden. The republic did not merely authorize force; it openly entered war. Millions were conscripted. Civilian life was reorganized. War was felt as a public condition. The declaration was not a formality. It was the legal and civic act by which the nation changed its condition.[172]

After World War II, the grammar of war began to change. Korea altered the doorway into war. Vietnam normalized the passage. The War Powers Resolution acknowledged the change without reversing it. The AUMF era completed the transition. The United States did not abandon war. It abandoned the older form by which war was publicly declared, bounded, and concluded.

Korea marked the eclipse of declaration in practice. The United States entered a major war under executive action and United Nations resolutions, followed by congressional appropriations and support, but not by formal declaration. Vietnam then showed what could happen when declaration disappeared and was replaced by a broad enabling resolution. The Gulf of Tonkin Resolution became a blank check, yet the draft ensured that the resulting war was still widely felt in the body of the republic. The War Powers Resolution was Congress's attempt to restore the old balance in statutory form, but its most effective lesson lay elsewhere: when Congress truly wished to stop a war, the hardest lever remained not consultation

---

[172] U.S. Senate Historical Office, "About Declarations of War by Congress"; Selective Service System, "Induction Statistics."

or reporting, but money. The purse remained the legislature's final weapon.[173]

Iran–Contra tested even that weapon. Congress had first authorized and funded a proxy war in Nicaragua, then withdrawn support through the Boland restrictions. Elements of the Executive then attempted to preserve the policy anyway, through covert channels, third-country assistance, private contributions, and diverted proceeds from the sale of U.S. arms to Iran. That episode did not only expose deception. It exposed how fragile legislative control becomes if appropriations can be circumvented. A republic cannot long preserve the meaning of congressional control over war if a determined executive can finance a prohibited policy outside the ordinary channels of law.[174]

The later decades revealed another transformation. The operational state no longer consisted only of a President and a military. Intelligence agencies, national-security staffs, covert-action procedures, proxy structures, and private contractors multiplied the channels through which force could be organized. The founders feared the concentration of war power in one magistrate. The modern republic faces a different but related danger: the diffusion of operational power through institutions whose secrecy, specialization, and overlapping jurisdictions make republican checks harder to apply. The problem is no longer simply a king-like President. It is a many-headed apparatus in which responsibility grows harder to see.

The AUMF era completed a further change in legal form. The 2001 and 2002 Authorizations for Use of Military Force did not declare war in the old sense. They authorized force broadly,

---

[173] *War Powers Resolution*, Pub. L. 93-148 (1973); Pub. L. 93-52, § 108, 87 Stat. 130 (1973).

[174] Report of the Congressional Committees Investigating the Iran–Contra Affair, S. Rep. No. 100-216 / H. Rep. No. 100-433 (1987).

tied it to executive determinations, and outlived the immediate crises that produced them. Successive administrations then interpreted those statutes across multiple theaters and many years. Congress still acted, but it did so once and broadly; the Executive then interpreted and operationalized the authority continuously. The republic remained constitutional. It also moved closer to living under a standing legal basis for war.[175]

At the same time, the social experience of war changed as much as the legal structure did.

The end of conscription in 1973 narrowed the military burden of war. The disappearance of broad economic mobilization narrowed the civilian burden. Earlier wars had demanded draft calls, rationing, war bond drives, industrial conversion, and visible shared sacrifice. After World War II, the United States retained a permanent defense establishment but not the older pattern of national mobilization. The all-volunteer force, joined to the permanent armaments economy, created a republic in which military action could continue for long periods without requiring most citizens to experience war as a direct rupture in ordinary life.[176]

**Perpetual emergency** is not sustained by law alone. It is sustained by a whole arrangement of political, institutional, economic, and civic conditions. Broad authorizations matter. Covert capabilities matter. Contractors matter. But equally important is a society in which war no longer demands general

---

[175] *Authorization for Use of Military Force*, Pub. L. 107-40 (2001); *Authorization for Use of Military Force Against Iraq Resolution of 2002*, Pub. L. 107-243; Report to Congress on the Legal and Policy Frameworks for the United States' Use of Military Force and Related National Security Operations (2024).

[176] Dwight D. Eisenhower, "Farewell Radio and Television Address to the American People," Jan. 17, 1961; Selective Service System, "Historical Timeline"; Richard Nixon, "Special Message to the Congress on Draft Reform," Apr. 23, 1970.

service, visible sacrifice, or widespread alteration of civilian life. A republic can live indefinitely in military action more easily when consent is occasional, burden is narrow, and attention itself is voluntary.

This is where Eisenhower's warning becomes newly intelligible. He went beyond the description of a large military establishment, to the birth of a permanent armaments economy and warned that its influence must be guarded against. The deeper implication was not simply economic. A permanent defense structure alters the rhythm of republican life. War becomes less an episode requiring mobilization and more a standing capability requiring management.

The result is not a dictatorship in the old Roman or Platonic sense. The United States still has elections, statutes, courts, appropriations, hearings, and public argument. The point is not that the republic has ceased to be constitutional. The point is that it has come to inhabit a different constitutional condition.

The founders assumed that war would be difficult to begin, visible when begun, and broadly felt once undertaken. The modern republic can now authorize force broadly, sustain it through standing institutions, conceal parts of it through covert means, privatize parts of it through contractors, and ask most citizens for neither compulsory service nor major economic sacrifice. In such a system, war becomes easier to normalize. Emergency ceases to look exceptional. The line between peace and war grows less distinct not because no line exists, but because the old public thresholds have weakened.

That is the answer toward which this book has been moving.

A republic can survive periods of emergency war. It can even survive long periods of war. What it cannot do without alteration is fight indefinitely while pretending that nothing fundamental has changed. The cost of perpetual emergency is not always visible in the forms of government. It appears in the relation between government and citizen, between law and force, between consent and burden, between public act and private operation.

The danger is not only that the executive becomes too powerful. It is also that war power becomes too normal, too procedural, too specialized, too dispersed, and too distant from the civic life of the people. A republic may then retain all the outward marks of constitutional order while slowly losing the older habit of peace.

The question, then, is not whether the United States can materially continue to fight. It plainly can. The question is whether a free government can live indefinitely in a state of managed, authorized, funded, covert, operationalized, and socially narrowed war without changing its own character.

It can fight forever.

What is far less certain is whether, in fighting forever, it can remain fully recognizable as a republic at peace.

# Appendices

# Appendices A through E
# Introduction

The pages that follow gather the principal documents, statutory milestones, and comparative tables on which the argument of this book rests.

They are not intended as an exhaustive catalogue of every military action undertaken by the United States. Their purpose is narrower, and it is hoped more useful: to place before the reader the constitutional forms through which the republic has entered, sustained, regulated, and ended war.

The appendices therefore serve as a companion to the narrative rather than a substitute for it. They present, in concentrated form, the formal declarations of war, the major modern authorizations for the use of force, the structure of the War Powers Resolution, and a comparative summary of how the constitutional grammar of war has changed over time.

Appendix A — *Declarations of War by the United States*
Appendix B — *Use of United States Armed Forces Abroad (1798-2023)*
Appendix C — *The War Powers Resolution*
Appendix D — *Major Authorizations for Use of Military Force*
Appendix E — *The Constitutional Grammar of War*

# Appendix A:
## Declarations of War by the United States

Congress has declared war on **eleven occasions**, across **five wars**, and its last formal declarations came during World War II. This appendix records those formal declarations only. It does not include later authorizations for the use of force, police actions, or other undeclared military conflicts, which are treated separately in the body of this book and in later appendices.

### *Formal Declarations of War*

| WAR | OPPONENT | DATE OF DECLARATION |
|---|---|---|
| War of 1812 | Great Britain | June 18, 1812 |
| Mexican–American War | Mexico | May 13, 1846 |
| Spanish–American War | Spain | April 25, 1898 |
| World War I | Germany | April 6, 1917 |
| World War I | Austria–Hungary | December 7, 1917 |
| World War II | Japan | December 8, 1941 |
| World War II | Germany | December 11, 1941 |
| World War II | Italy | December 11, 1941 |
| World War II | Bulgaria | June 5, 1942 |
| World War II | Hungary | June 5, 1942 |
| World War II | Rumania | June 5, 1942 |

The constitutional significance of this list lies not merely in its brevity, but in its endpoint. After June 1942, Congress did not again use the formal declaration as the nation's public legal doorway into major war. What followed was not the disappearance of congressional participation, but a change in its form: resolutions, appropriations, and later Authorizations for Use of Military Force replaced the older declaration model. That transition is one of the central themes of this book.

*Source note:* Dates compiled from the official Senate history of declarations of war and the codified list of U.S. declarations of war. For original document texts and document images, see the U.S. Senate declarations archive and the National Archives milestone documents.

# Appendix B:
## Use of United States
## Armed Forces Abroad (1798-2023)

The United States Constitution gives Congress the authority "to declare War," while designating the President as Commander in Chief of the armed forces. In practice, however, the relationship between these powers has evolved far beyond the limited concept of formally declared wars.

To help Congress understand this evolution, the Congressional Research Service (CRS) periodically compiles a comprehensive historical record titled *Instances of Use of United States Armed Forces Abroad* (Report R42738). The purpose of the report is not to interpret the Constitution or judge the legality of any action, but simply to document the occasions when American military forces have been used outside the United States. The list assists Congress in evaluating war-powers legislation, oversight responsibilities, and the broader historical context of presidential and congressional authority over military action.

The CRS report reveals a striking fact. While the United States has issued only **11 formal declarations** of war in its history (covering five conflicts), the CRS record identifies **481** instances in which U.S. armed forces were used abroad between **1798 and April 2023**. These instances include wars, limited military strikes, peacekeeping missions, evacuations of American citizens, and short-term deployments during international crises.

The contrast between formal declarations of war and the much larger number of military actions illustrates the gradual transformation of American war powers. Over time, the United

States moved from a system in which war was formally declared to one in which military force is frequently employed without such declarations.

*What Counts as an "Instance"*

The CRS list uses a deliberately broad definition of military action. Entries include:

- Declared wars
- Limited combat operations
- Naval and air strikes
- Peacekeeping deployments
- Military interventions during crises
- Evacuations of American citizens from unstable regions

The list does not include routine overseas basing, training missions, or most covert operations. The goal is to record situations where U.S. forces were actively employed in response to a crisis or conflict abroad.

*A Long View of American Military Action*

When the CRS data is viewed across time, it reveals a clear pattern: the frequency of U.S. military actions abroad has steadily increased.

| Historical Period | Approximate Instances | Average per Decade |
|---|---|---|
| 1798–1899 | ~75 | ~7 |
| 1900–1945 | ~95 | ~21 |
| 1946–1990 | ~150 | ~33 |
| 1991–2023 | ~160 | ~50 |

*Appendix B: Use of United States Armed Forces Abroad*

*The Early Republic (1798–1899)*

In the nineteenth century the United States used military force abroad only occasionally. Most actions involved protecting American commerce or citizens overseas. Examples include naval operations against the Barbary states, anti-piracy patrols, and limited interventions in Latin America or East Asia. Military actions during this period were relatively infrequent.

*The Rise of an Overseas Power (1900–1945)*

After the Spanish-American War of 1898 the United States became an overseas power with new strategic interests. American forces were repeatedly deployed in the Caribbean and Central America, and expeditionary forces appeared in China and elsewhere. The period also includes the nation's entry into World War I and World War II. The number of interventions increased substantially compared with the nineteenth century.

*The Cold War Era (1946–1990)*

Following World War II, the United States assumed a permanent global security role. Military actions abroad included major wars in Korea and Vietnam, as well as numerous smaller interventions and crisis deployments tied to Cold War tensions. The United States maintained military commitments across Europe, Asia, and the Middle East, and the frequency of military actions increased again.

*The Post-Cold War Era (1991–2023)*

After the collapse of the Soviet Union the United States remained the world's dominant military power. Operations during this period included the Gulf War, interventions in the Balkans, operations in Afghanistan and Iraq, and numerous counterterrorism deployments, air strikes, and evacuations. The pace of military actions reached its highest level in this era.

## A Striking Historical Observation

From 1798 through 2023—a span of approximately **226 years** — the United States employed military force abroad in **207 of those years**. In other words, American forces have been engaged overseas in the vast majority of years since the nation's early history.

Yet only five conflicts in that entire period were formally declared wars.

## The Significance of the CRS Record

The CRS list does not attempt to judge whether particular uses of force were justified or constitutional. Instead, it provides a historical foundation for understanding how American war powers have evolved.

The record illustrates the central tension explored in this book:

The constitutional system was designed around formal declarations of war, yet the modern United States frequently employs military force without such declarations. Over time, the nation has moved from a model of war by declaration to one characterized increasingly by military action under continuing emergency authorities.

Understanding this historical pattern is essential for evaluating the modern American approach to war powers and the ongoing debate over the proper balance between Congress and the presidency.

# Appendix C:
## The War Powers Resolution

The **War Powers Resolution** of 1973 was Congress's most direct statutory effort to restore a measure of constitutional balance after Korea and Vietnam. It did not revive the older declaration model. Instead, it attempted to regulate the modern pattern in which presidents might introduce United States forces into hostilities first and Congress would then respond through consultation, reporting, authorization, or withdrawal. The statute remains codified at 50 U.S.C. §§ 1541–1548.

The Resolution states that its purpose is to ensure that the **"collective judgment"** of both Congress and the President applies to the introduction of United States armed forces into hostilities or into situations where imminent involvement in hostilities is clearly indicated. It further provides that the President's constitutional power to introduce such forces is exercised only pursuant to **(1) a declaration of war, (2) specific statutory authorization, or (3) a national emergency created by attack upon the United States, its territories or possessions, or its armed forces**.
The core provisions are these:

### 1. Consultation

The President must consult with Congress "in every possible instance" before introducing United States armed forces into hostilities or into situations where imminent involvement in hostilities is clearly indicated, and must continue to consult regularly thereafter until the forces are no longer engaged or have been removed.

## 2. Reporting within Forty-Eight Hours

Absent a declaration of war, the President must submit a written report within **48 hours** whenever United States armed forces are introduced

(1) into hostilities or situations where imminent involvement in hostilities is clearly indicated;

(2) into the territory, airspace, or waters of a foreign nation while equipped for combat, except for deployments relating solely to supply, replacement, repair, or training; or

(3) in numbers that substantially enlarge combat-equipped forces already located in a foreign nation.

The report must set forth the circumstances, the constitutional and legislative authority relied upon, and the estimated scope and duration of the hostilities or involvement.

## 3. The Sixty-Day Clock

Within **60 days** after a report is submitted — or required to be submitted — the President must terminate the use of armed forces unless Congress has declared war, enacted specific authorization, extended the period by law, or is physically unable to meet because of armed attack. The statute permits one additional **30-day extension** if the President certifies that unavoidable military necessity requires continued use of force to ensure the safe removal of U.S. forces.

## 4. Congressional Direction to Remove Forces

Section 5(c), as enacted in 1973, provided that forces engaged in hostilities without declaration or specific statutory authorization "shall be removed by the President if the Congress so directs by concurrent resolution." That mechanism reflected Congress's attempt to preserve a relatively quick legislative check on continuing hostilities.

### 5. No Implied Authorization

Section 8 is especially important. It provides that authority to introduce U.S. forces into hostilities shall not be inferred from any provision of law, including an appropriation act, unless the provision specifically authorizes such introduction and states that it is intended to constitute specific statutory authorization under the Resolution. Nor may such authority be inferred from a treaty unless the treaty is implemented by legislation specifically authorizing hostilities.

The War Powers Resolution therefore did not abolish executive initiative. It tried to place executive initiative inside a statutory framework of consultation, reporting, and termination. That is why it occupies such a central place in the constitutional history of modern American war powers. It represents Congress's attempt to discipline a practice that had already moved away from declaration.

One part of that framework later became constitutionally doubtful. In **INS v. Chadha** (1983), the Supreme Court held that a legislative veto mechanism lacking presidential presentment violated the Constitution's requirements for legislative action. Although *Chadha* involved a one-house veto rather than the War Powers Resolution itself, the decision cast serious doubt on Section 5(c)'s use of a **concurrent resolution** to compel withdrawal without presentation to the President. A concurrent resolution passes both houses of Congress but is not presented for presidential signature or veto.

For that reason, the most enduring practical force of the Resolution has lain less in its original concurrent-resolution device than in its reporting requirements, its sixty-day framework, and its continuing role in structuring the constitutional argument between Congress and the President. The statute did not restore the old grammar of declared war. It created the legal architecture within which much of the later undeclared use of force would be contested.

# Appendix D:
## Major Authorizations for Use of Military Force (AUMFs)

Below are the principal modern statutes by which Congress authorized large-scale military force without using the older form of formal declaration.

### *Major Congressional Authorizations*

1.  **Gulf of Tonkin Resolution**

    Joint Resolution to Promote the Maintenance of International Peace and Security in Southeast Asia

    Approved August 10, 1964

    Public Law 88-408

    This resolution authorized the President "to take all necessary measures to repel any armed attack against the forces of the United States and to prevent further aggression" in Southeast Asia. It became the principal statutory basis for the later expansion of the Vietnam War.

2.  **Authorization for Use of Military Force Against Iraq Resolution**

    Approved January 14, 1991

    Public Law 102-1

    This joint resolution authorized the President to use United States armed forces pursuant to United Nations Security Council Resolution 678 in order to implement prior Security Council resolutions concerning Iraq's invasion of Kuwait. It marked a major modern instance of congressional authorization for war short of declaration.

3. **Authorization for Use of Military Force**

Approved September 18, 2001

Public Law 107-40

This joint resolution authorized the President to use "all necessary and appropriate force" against those nations, organizations, or persons he determined had planned, authorized, committed, or aided the attacks of September 11, 2001, or harbored those responsible. More than any other modern statute, it became the foundation of a continuing and geographically expansive war authorization.

4. **Authorization for Use of Military Force Against Iraq Resolution of 2002**

Approved October 16, 2002

Public Law 107-243

This resolution authorized the President to use the armed forces "as he determines to be necessary and appropriate" to defend the national security of the United States against the continuing threat posed by Iraq and to enforce relevant United Nations Security Council resolutions. It provided the domestic statutory basis for the 2003 Iraq War.

These authorizations do not erase Congress from the constitutional story of war. On the contrary, they show Congress remaining present, but in a different legal form. The declaration of war once marked a public constitutional change in the nation's condition. The modern authorization permits force while leaving the republic, at least formally, short of that older and more visible threshold. That shift — from declaration to authorization — is one of the central developments traced throughout this book.

# Appendix E:
## The Constitutional Grammar of War

The chapters of this book have examined American war powers through five recurring questions:

1. **Authority** — by what claimed authority was force initiated, widened, or sustained?
2. **Assent** — what form of congressional or public consent existed?
3. **Visibility** — how visible was the action to Congress and to the public?
4. **Burden** — how widely were the costs distributed across the citizen body?
5. **Termination** — by what mechanism was force limited, ended, or brought back under ordinary constitutional conditions?

The table below is not an exhaustive catalogue of American military actions. It is a comparative summary of several major episodes discussed in this book, intended to show how the constitutional grammar of war changed over time.

### *Comparative Table of Constitutional War Practice*

| CONFLICT / EPISODE | AUTHORITY | ASSENT | VISIBILITY | BURDEN | TERMINATION |
|---|---|---|---|---|---|
| **Barbary War (1801–1805)** | Presidential defensive naval action, later widened by congressional statute | Congressional authorization short of declaration | Public naval conflict | Narrow military burden; limited civilian disruption | Treaty with Tripoli |

| Conflict / Episode | Authority | Assent | Visibility | Burden | Termination |
|---|---|---|---|---|---|
| **Mexican–American War (1846–1848)** | Congressional declaration of war | Formal declaration | Fully public war | Volunteers and regular army; visible but limited national mobilization | Treaty of Guadalupe Hidalgo |
| **World War I (1917–1918)** | Congressional declaration | Formal declaration after prolonged neutrality debate | Fully public war | Draft, industrial mobilization, war finance | Armistice and treaty settlement |
| **World War II (1941–1945)** | Congressional declarations after direct attack | Formal declarations and overwhelming public assent | Total public war | Draft, rationing, war bonds, industrial conversion | Surrender of Axis powers |
| **Korea (1950–1953)** | Presidential action under U.N. resolutions | Congressional appropriations and political support, but no declaration | Public war, but without declaration | Draft continued; broad but less total burden than WWII | Armistice |
| **Vietnam (1964–1975)** | Gulf of Tonkin Resolution and executive escalation | Broad congressional authorization, later eroding political support | Highly visible war | Draft, deferments, protest, broad civic friction | Congressional repeal, withdrawal, and funding cutoff |
| **Iran–Contra (1984–1986)** | Covert executive action after congressional restrictions | Congress had earlier funded policy, then restricted it through Boland | Secret or semi-secret; public policy and covert policy diverged | Narrow burden; costs concentrated in covert apparatus and proxy forces | Exposure, investigations, prosecutions, renewed congressional assertion |
| **Post-9/11 conflicts (2001– )** | 2001 AUMF, later extended through executive interpretation | Broad statutory authorization; no declaration | Mixed: overt campaigns, covert action, classified operations | Volunteer military, contractors, limited civic and economic mobilization | No clear constitutional closure; conflict becomes ongoing |

## Observations

Several broad changes emerge from this comparison.

**First, declaration gives way to authorization.**
The older constitutional act by which the republic openly changed its condition gradually disappears. In its place stand resolutions, authorizations, and executive interpretations.

**Second, visibility declines.**

Earlier wars were openly declared and publicly experienced. Later conflicts often combine overt military action with covert, proxy, or classified operations.

**Third, burden narrows.**

Earlier wars required broad military or economic mobilization. The modern republic relies increasingly on volunteers, contractors, debt, and specialized institutions.

**Fourth, termination becomes less clear.**

Formal declarations and treaties once marked the entry into and exit from war more visibly. In the modern system, conflicts are often limited by armistice, funding decisions, administrative reinterpretation, or simply allowed to continue.

The constitutional grammar of war has therefore not disappeared. It has changed. The republic still authorizes, funds, and conducts force. But it does so through forms that are less public, less singular, and less closely tied to the civic burden once associated with war.

# Index

## E



## F



## G



## H



## I



## J



## K



## L

## U



## V



## W

www.ingramcontent.com/pod-product-compliance
Lightning Source LLC
Chambersburg PA
CBHW051434130726
47987CB00005B/2039